PRASE FOR

At Home in this Life: Finding Peace at the Crossroads
of Unraveled Dreams & Beautiful Surprises

"In a world where social media encourages perfection through retouched photos and happy highlights, we need truth tellers like Jerusalem Jackson Greer. *At Home in this Life* reminds the reader that, though our lives are not perfect, they are still beautiful. It is a joy to read, like sitting down with a good friend, comparing notes and saying, 'Yes, exactly. I'm so glad I found you.'"

—Traci Smith, author of *Faithful Families*

"Hope deferred makes the heart sick" (Prov. 13:12). *At Home in this Life* is tonic for what ails us. Its stories, recipes, and projects add up to a comforting but instructive lesson in how to make a home and find peace in the seasons before our dreams come true. Who knew that waiting could be so beautiful or taste so good? Embracing a range of home-centered pursuits, from gardening to serving the homeless, *At Home in this Life* is exactly my kind of page-turner. I loved this book."

—Christie Purifoy, author of *Roots & Sky*

"Many of us long for a more whole, beautiful, and ordered life and imagine that a change in our circumstances might bring about what we desire. Jerusalem invites us on the journey she's traveled, with humility, honesty, and humor, to transformation through practices firmly rooted in the lives we already have. She offers hope that a new way is possible and a tangible example of learning to faithfully love what is right in front of us!"

—Mark and Lisa Scandrette, authors of *Belonging and Becoming* and *Free*

"This book is for all of us who have struggled to embrace the imperfect reality of our present moment. The author weaves her own ordinary story with the wisdom of St. Benedict's rule, and in doing so invites us all into the gifts of stability, service to one another, and as she says, 'cooperation with God in my own transformation.' Her story of everyday transformation is one we all need to hear again and again."

—Micha Boyett, Author of *Found: A Story of Questions, Grace, and Everyday Prayer*

"I love Jerusalem's realness, her willingness to walk us through her own story and show us how it mimics a universal story we all know in our bones: God is good, even when things end up differently than how we thought they would. Her wit, candor, and love of ancient practices woke up my bones to a renewed sense of wonder at how God is at work around us all the time, in ways big and small. Her ordinary life is a gift, because it's full of the magic of God—just like all our lives."

—Tsh Oxenreider, author of *At Home in the World* and *Notes From a Blue Bike*

"Jerusalem Jackson Greer has written a relatable, warm, and utterly charming book of theology within time and place. The radical act of staying put with a community and a home and a family is an example of faith and hope and healing for these fragmented instant times. This is an incarnational book, an embodiment of how God shows up in our right-now lives with steady surprise and everyday richness."

—Sarah Bessey, author of *Out of Sorts: Making Peace with an Evolving Faith*

"The author writes with poignant conviction about the best of life—that moment when we surrender our roots to the earth for the long haul. Weaving profound truths with ordinary home-keeping tasks, she reminds us that all is sacred and God is vibrantly alive in our mundane. This book is a hopeful liturgy of endurance, even for the city-dweller like me."

—Shannan Martin, Author of *Falling Free: Rescued from the Life I Always Wanted*

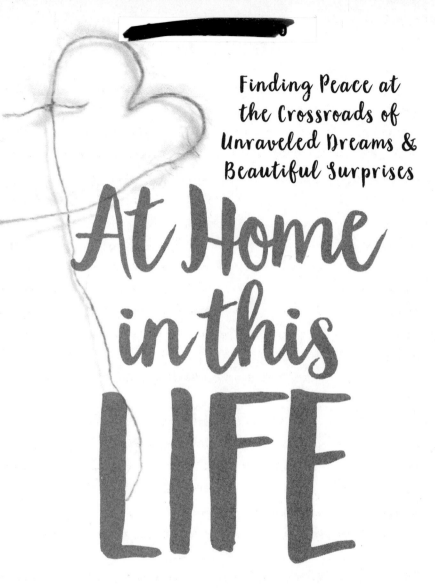

Finding Peace at
the Crossroads of
Unraveled Dreams &
Beautiful Surprises

At Home
in this
LIFE

Jerusalem Jackson Greer

PARACLETE PRESS
BREWSTER, MASSACHUSETTS

2017 First Printing

At Home in This Life: Finding Peace at the Crossroads of Unraveled Dreams & Beautiful Surprises

ISBN 978-1-61261-632-2

Scripture quotations marked (MSG) are taken from *The Message*. Copyright © 1993, 1994, 1995, 1996, 2000, 2001, 2002. Used by permission of NavPress Publishing Group.

Scripture quotations marked (NRSV) are from the New Revised Standard Version Bible, copyright © 1989 the Division of Christian Education of the National Council of the Churches of Christ in the United States of America. Used by permission. All rights reserved.

Scripture quotations marked (NLT) are taken from the Holy Bible, New Living Translation, copyright © 1996, 2004, 2007 by Tyndale House Foundation. Used by permission of Tyndale House Publishers, Inc., Carol Stream, Illinois 60188. All rights reserved.

Scripture designated (VOICE) taken from The Voice™ Copyright © 2008 by Ecclesia Bible Society. Used by permission. All rights reserved.

Scripture quotations marked (NIV) are taken from the Holy Bible, New International Version®, NIV® Copyright © 1973, 1978, 1984, 2011 by Biblica, Inc.™ Used by permission of Zondervan. All rights reserved worldwide. www.zondervan.com The "NIV" and "New International Version" are trademarks registered in the United States Patent and Trademark Office by Biblica, Inc.™

Scripture quotations marked (CEB) are taken from the Common English Bible®, CEB® Copyright © 2010, 2011 by Common English Bible.™ Used by permission. All rights reserved worldwide. The "CEB" and "Common English Bible" trademarks are registered in the United States Patent and Trademark Office by Common English Bible. Use of either trademark requires the permission of Common English Bible.

Unless otherwise specified, quotations in English from The Rule of St. Benedict are taken from *The Rule of St. Benedict in English*, ed. Timothy Fry (New York: Vintage Books, 1998).

The Paraclete Press name and logo (dove on cross) are trademarks of Paraclete Press, Inc.

Library of Congress Cataloging-in-Publication Data

Names: Greer, Jerusalem Jackson, author.
Title: At home in this life : finding peace at the crossroads of unraveled
   dreams & beautiful surprises / Jerusalem Jackson Greer.
Description: Brewster MA : Paraclete Press Inc., 2017. | Includes
   bibliographical references.
Identifiers: LCCN 2017005061 | ISBN 9781612616322
Subjects: LCSH: Greer, Jerusalem Jackson, author. | Christian biography.
Classification: LCC BR1725.G79 A3 2017 | DDC 277.3/083092 [B] --dc23
LC record available at https://lccn.loc.gov/2017005061

10 9 8 7 6 5 4 3 2 1

Published by Paraclete Press
Brewster, Massachusetts
www.paracletepress.com
Printed in the United States of America

To Phyllis,

My fairy godmother, my patron saint, my friend.

I miss you so.

May today there be peace within.

May you trust God that you are exactly where you are meant to be.

May you not forget the infinite possibilities that are born of faith.

May you use those gifts that you have received, and pass on the love that has been given to you.

May you be content knowing you are a child of God.

Let this presence settle into your bones, and allow your soul the freedom to sing, dance, praise, and love.

It is there for each and every one of us.

—Teresa of Avila

Contents

Part 4: Spreading Out

Foreword

There are books that are largely collections of ideas—head books, brain books, concept books. Honestly, those aren't my kinds of books. My kind of book is the one about life and dreams and farms and feet and bread and kids and marriage—and all the ways that faith informs and weaves through and is challenged and deepened by all those other parts of our life. This is that kind of book. This is my kind of book.

In my experience, the most seismic changes in my heart and my faith occur right within the warp and woof of daily, ordinary life. This is a book about that—about how our longings and disappointments can become the soil in which our faith is brought further to life.

Jerusalem and I are kindred in many ways—we both value hospitality in our bones, believing that gathering people in our homes and around our tables is sacred, beautiful work. And another way we're similar—we hold an idea in our minds of what life should be, what our life should be, what would make everything just perfect, and then we kick and scream when life, inevitably, doesn't obey our commands.

I lived a season much like the one you'll discover in these pages—a heartbreak over a house, a fracture of faith, a season where everything in our life seemed stuck and muddy. As much as I hate for this to be true, these seasons are invitations: to get over ourselves, to ask for help, to dwell more deeply with God, to be transformed into the better, wholer versions of ourselves.

If you find yourself aching for a life just beyond your reality—whether that's a farm or a baby or a marriage or a house or whatever, you will find in these pages an honest friend and a life-changing truth: your ache and longing will be the tools of your transformation, right exactly where you are.

Shauna Niequist

Introduction

That faith and love operate best through the humble means of boring,
everyday occupations is a thoroughly biblical perspective,
for its stories repeatedly remind us that God's attention is fixed
on what we regard as unimportant and unworthy.
—Kathleen Norris

At this juncture in life, knowing what I know, and blissfully unaware of what I don't know, I have come to the following conclusion: balance, when it comes to living a wholehearted life, is a myth. It is a beautiful myth sold to us by advertising agencies, planner companies (oh, I love the hunt for the magic planner!), and storage solution stores. And over time, this myth has morphed into an idol many of us chase. An idol we believe will make us whole, make our lives more sane and our days more calm. But while I adore the thought of living a nice, steady, evenly balanced life, I am convinced than the relentless pursuit of this ideal is at best like chasing after a fairytale, and at worst a dangerous distraction from being present to the life we have.

To be sure, some balance and harmony are promised in the depth and breadth of spiritual practices such as silence and solitude, prayer and reflection. That all sounds lovely, right? Except that as a busy, working, creative mother, stepping away from daily life for the sort of time prescribed by most monastic disciplines and practices has always been out of the question. While I see the value in long periods of silence, days upon days of retreats, and a closet just for praying, my kids, my job, and the mortgage company find them much less enchanting. And, honestly, I have trouble with the idea of fitting "one more thing" into my already busy schedule. I want spiritual practices that will help me live a slower version of my modern life—practicing the presence of God right where I am—not adding another impossible standard of perfection to the top of my already full to-do list. I bet you feel this way too.

We all live smack in the middle of beauty and mess, and much to our dismay there is no product or app that can prepare us for, or insulate us from, the mess. We know from experience, you and I, that when messy things enter our lives—the broken feet, the lost house sales, the chicken massacres, the sick children, the lost jobs—they do not wait for an invitation. They do not wait until the laundry is done, until the checkbook is balanced, or until the kitchen floor is clean. They come and wedge themselves right in between the never-ending demands of daily life—the drama of the carpool line, the stack of bills already too high, and the career we have but don't always love. They come in the midst of births and deaths, celebrations and seasons of depression. They arrive when things are good and when things are worse. They come with balloons and with shut-off notices.

So how then do we live? What are we to do?

The somewhat dismaying (or perhaps comforting?) truth is that Scripture is full of examples of people living this same way—right at the crossroads of unraveled dreams and beautiful surprises. Lives full of disaster and delight, celebration and mourning, sickness and healing, ordinary and extraordinary moments, all crashing into each other despite the best-laid plans. Nowhere is there an emphasis on living a balanced life. Instead, the lessons I glean from the stories of David, Ruth, Timothy, Esther, Noah, and from the lives of the saints who have gone before us—Francis, Benedict, Theresa, Lottie Moon—are not ones of how to create a foolproof plan for a balanced life. Instead I find example after example of a life thrown into chaos, trampled and muddied by unpredictable circumstances, strong emotions, and challenging relationships, punctuated with beauty and healing.

It is in one of these seasons for me—a season filled with striving for balance while ignoring the gaping holes in my heart—that my dreams dramatically unraveled. In this season, the Holy Spirit began (again!) to help me release my selfish and controlling agenda for my life, and replace it with a new agenda, a new life, a wholehearted life, rooted in love, service, stewardship, and transformation—a way of being in the world that would require me to stretch and grow and stay and learn.

What follows in these chapters is the story of how everything I thought would make me happy came undone, and then how I found a way to make myself at home in this beautiful, messy, amazingly tender, completely unbalanced life, by imperfectly practicing one spiritual discipline at a time—smack in the middle of raising the kids, mending the sweaters, and burning the bread.

Jerusalem Jackson Greer

PART 1

GOING

chapter 1

Mess

If we pay attention to our tears, they'll show us something about ourselves.
—Shauna Niequist, *Bread and Wine*

There is a certain freedom in being unstable. In always being on the move, chasing dreams, laying out new plans. After all, who doesn't love a search for the greener grass, the pot of gold, the lucky strike? We know it must be out there, we have seen signs of it on Instagram and Pinterest. In our search for The Next Thing, some of us shed places and people like last year's winter coat. We blow up our lives time and time again, leaving a cloud of dust that no one can see through long enough to catch us, always watching for the moment when we can jump on the next train to Something New or Somewhere Different. And then there is the more socially acceptable approach of escape practiced by the tribe I belong to. We have a different, slower way of leaving. Sometimes we even try to implicate God in our plans to change, move, leave, abandon, quit, and run. "We are just being who we were created to be," we say. "We are just following God's call on our lives," we explain. "God has closed this door, but I am sure there is a window open somewhere," we rationalize as we scoot out the back door, our excuses spilling out of our hastily packed suitcases. We are the ones who are always waiting for our lives to start, the ones who work overtime creating a smoke screen of contentment, so no one will suspect that we are actually biding our time, waiting for the all-elusive *Someday When* to show up and save us.

You have heard about *Someday When*, right?

Someday When we move *we will all get along better.*

Someday When I change jobs *I won't be so tired or cranky at home.*

Someday When I lose weight *I will take my kids to the pool.*

Someday When we have enough money *I won't be so controlling.*

Someday When I find the right church *I will be happier.*

Someday When we have kids *I will be fulfilled.*

Once upon a time, not so many years ago, I was living a life that I didn't want. I was living in a house I didn't want, in a town I didn't want to live in, working at a job I didn't want to have. I was burned out, exhausted, and weary, and every edge of my being was frayed beyond recognition. If my life had been a Lifetime movie it would have been called *Biting Off More Than She Can Chew.* And all around me was the proof—my house was a disaster, and I was constantly sick with colds and fevers from my overcommitting ways.

It was during this season that my friend Shauna tweeted the following: "Exhaustion is not a badge of honor I want to wear anymore." I read that comment, cheered for her, re-tweeted it (and watched as it was then re-tweeted more than anything I have ever quoted before or since), then promptly succumbed to an exhaustion-induced cold that landed me in bed for a week. Lying in bed, staring at the dust on my ceiling fan, chastising myself for its presence, too worn out and sickly to do anything about it, I was comforted to know I was not alone in my exhaustion or my conviction that all this busyness was (a) getting me nowhere and (b) highly overrated as a sign of wonder-womanliness.

Of course once I had recovered from the flat-on-my-back cold, it wasn't long before I was up to my old habits again. Doing too much, expecting too much, pushing too hard, and hating my life (and ultimately myself) for it. Overwhelmed by the mess of my life, I came up with a plan—a plan to change everything, a plan to fix everything that was broken. The plan was this: I would run as fast as I could into a different life. And that different life would be the life of a farm gal. A life that would be slower, gentler, less frenetic. A life of walks in the orchard, fishing in the pond, and picnics in the fields.

My awareness that I wanted to live in the country can be traced directly to a woman named Phyllis Tickle. I discovered Phyllis in Barnes & Noble on an autumn Tuesday morning. I remember that it was a Tuesday because I always went to B&N after yoga, which was always on Tuesdays. So there I was, at the big box bookstore, taking my sweet time combing through the sale section, doing my best to avoid going home to piles of dirty dishes and even dirtier laundry when I bumped into Phyllis on the Last Chance bargain cart. To this day I am not sure why I bought Phyllis's memoir, *The Shaping of a Life*. I cannot remember what it was that called to me from the dust jacket synopsis, but this one little four-dollar discovery would completely and utterly change the trajectory of my life. And that is not hyperbole. I can say with all confidence that you would not be reading my words right now if I had not procrastinated about my laundry that day.

I was as hooked on Phyllis as I had been on Anne Shirley of Green Gables at the age of twelve, even though I was as far removed at thirty-two from this Tennessee doctor's wife and academic mother of seven as I had been from a Canadian orphan living on Prince Edward Island then. Yet in both instances there had been a recognition, a reflection of self that was undeniable. Somewhere in the middle of

Phyllis's words I found a part of myself that had until that moment been lying dormant, and the awakening was so acute that I have never recovered from it.

Aware of my newfound love, my sweet husband tracked down all three volumes of her *Farm in Lucy* series (books that weren't easy to come by in our little town in the pre-Amazon Prime era) for Christmas gifts that year. This small series follows the rhythm of the liturgical year through stories of the Tickles' family life on a small farm in Lucy, Tennessee, stories that are filled with equal doses of charm and wisdom.

As I sat in bed that cold December, reading Phyllis's *What the Land Already Knows*, tears began to stream down my face. And I was only on the prologue. But it was the prologue that would change everything.

Phyllis and her husband Sam's decision to move their family out of the city and into the country came about because they had come to the conclusion that their seven children did not know how to grow and tend, make and make do, or understand the true cost of living. Phyllis wrote that her kids "also possessed none of the freedom or discipline that come from knowing how to live on the land. Ultimately, it is always the land and what it knows that sustain life; and it was to the land that we had to take them before it was too late." This passage appears in the prologue for each *Farm in Lucy* volume, and every time I would read it I would cry, a river of tears streaming down my face uncontrollably. And I had no idea why.

In a recent conversation with a friend about how she knew it was time to pursue her calling to become an Episcopal priest, she said the fact that she cried at every ordination service she attended was a bit of a tip-off that her time had come to follow suit. I have never cried in an ordination service (though I have sat and waited to see if I would), but each and every time I would read Phyllis's prologue (and I read these books seasonally), the waterworks were turned on and my heart felt as if it would come out of my body with longing. The only explanation of those tears that ever made sense is this: those books, and in particular that passage, awoke a desire in me that I never even knew I had. A light switch had been flipped in a previously undiscovered room of my heart. This longing for a life I didn't understand, for which I had no context and almost no vocabulary, was now pulsing through my heart. A conversion had begun. And to complicate matters, my husband, Nathan, was also experiencing a conversion of the same sort, in his own way. We were being called to the land, and it was to the land that we knew we had to take our family (though we couldn't yet articulate why) before it was too late. It would only take us a decade to get there.

When we first felt the call to a more rural sort of life, we had just bought the house we thought would be our forever home, a lovely 1940s fixer-upper cottage in a historic neighborhood that I had long dreamed of living in. We had two small children, a ton of debt, and no idea who or what we wanted to be when we grew up. And even though our hearts were being pulled to a different way of life, a way of life we couldn't even name yet, we knew we were not going anywhere anytime soon. The truth was we had boxed ourselves in, and it was going to take some time to find a way out. There were a lot of other dreams that had to be pursued and mistakes that had to be made first. Besides, what did we know of this longing, this itch, this calling, other than what my tears told me, what Nathan's longing to work the land told him? Those were the years before hobby farming, smallholding sustainability, and hipster homesteading were common. No one in our circle was attempting this sort of life; there was no one we could look to for guidance or wisdom about how one goes from a city life to a country life with very little experience and even less capital.

And so we shoved this longing to the back of our hearts, in the drawer where we stuff all the things we call Crazy Ideas, and went about raising our kids, going to work, pursuing other dreams, and working on the house. Over the next few years our life was full of outward signs of forward motion. We survived toddlerhood. I started a business, lost a business, and got a job. Nathan was promoted, the kids started school, and we changed churches a few times. I received my first book contract, our house was featured in a national magazine, and Nathan's band won a local contest. I was able to co-pastor a church, and the boys got into a great new school. We checked off box after box on our bucket list, but neither of us ever felt completely settled. We did the sorts of things that you do when trying to numb the aching hole in your heart: we ate too much, drank too much, slept too much, worked too much, ignored too much. We ran up more debt, we played a lovely round or two of My Unhappiness Is Your Fault, and we spent a lot of time in our therapist's office—together and apart. An annoying cloud of angst and dissatisfaction seemed to trail behind us like a piece of toilet paper on the bottom of a shoe.

A compounding issue in those years was Nathan's progressive unhappiness and the ways he chose to cope with the increasingly dark cloud over him. It was akin in some ways to acedia, that spiritual and mental apathy that can come from a life of deep repetition and little meaning. We now understand that the darkness was a combination (in his words) of "a really bad attitude and an even worse diagnosis." But in the deep, thick middle of it, before the medical stuff was sorted out (severe sleep apnea, adult onset of attention deficit disorder), and before Nathan had his own come-to-Jesus, palm-to-forehead, attitude-adjusting moment, his unhappiness was the fifth and often neediest member of our family, a member whose mood—distant or short-tempered—could change the tone of any given day. I felt it was my job to manage this presence; I worked overtime to push it back from consuming our home life.

I'm a solutions person. I like to think that there is always a solution. My personality is wired so that I am on a constant search to make life better—for myself, my family, my friends. I love to improve any situation and I am a tad obsessed with the idea of personal growth. Of course there are many benefits and pitfalls to being this sort of person. The benefits include being good at handling chaos and being a quick problem solver; but a major pitfall is that I put a lot of stock in Movement versus Waiting. All too often, I would rather slap a Band-Aid on a problem than allow the space, time, and discomfort that true healing needs, especially if this in any way outwardly resembles Doing Nothing, as I have very little patience for the appearance of stagnation.

During those years, I slapped on a lot of Band-Aids. Nathan's deep dissatisfaction with his career path was a puzzle I took upon myself to solve because he could not (or would not as it seemed at times).

I have often described our marriage as being akin to "The Tortoise and the Hare": he being the tortoise and me the hare. I am always ready to try something new, start a new project, jump off into a new idea, run around in circles of inspiration and ideas until I crash, overwhelmed and exhausted. Nathan is always ready to wait. He is an excellent plodder. He is a master at staying the course, at finishing what he starts. But his tortoise tendencies also mean that he is never quick to make a change, and risk is not his friend. Nathan prefers to see the end of the road before he steps out on the path, while I am perhaps a little too quick to run into the road before I look both ways.

The career path Nathan had fallen into did not feed his soul, but it did provide us with a respectable, solid income, and good benefits. Nathan believed in the "Get on a payroll, and stay on a payroll" mantra, even if the payroll was one he hated. (His steady, plodding ways did provide me a lot of freedom for exploring a never-ending stream of new ideas.) And while I respected him immensely for sacrificing his happiness for ours, I also deeply resented him for it. Living with an unhappy person, no matter how noble the reason is for their unhappiness, is still difficult.

So I helped with job searches, encouraged career change options, found new doctors, lobbied for new medicines, and encouraged him to join a new band and play gigs whenever he could. And all the while I asked, week after week, year after year after year: "What do you want to do with your life? What would make you happy? Just tell me and we will do it. Whatever it is, we will find a way to make it happen."

Over time, thanks to a great therapist, Nathan's willing spirit, and better and better diagnoses, things did improve. (Side note: It is amazing how a person can change once they get the rest they need, once they have someone on their side who will take the time to listen and diagnose properly.) The dark cloud started to shrink. But the question of what would make Nathan truly happy remained unanswered, and my desperation to do whatever I could to ensure a happy home grew.

chapter 2

The Plan

> The great thing, if one can, is to stop regarding all the unpleasant things as interruptions of one's "own," or "real" life. The truth is of course that what one calls the interruptions are precisely one's real life—the life God is sending one day by day.
> —C. S. Lewis

One cold, wintry weekend, we went to visit our friends Ben and Jeanetta at their home just outside of town. They live in a lovely cabin-esque house on a wooded hill on two acres complete with goats and chickens in their yard. We had gone to see them only intending to stay for dinner. Almost as soon as we arrived, however, the snow began to fall, and we found ourselves bedded down at Darley Farm for the weekend.

During that weekend Nathan and Ben spent the majority of their time outside, hunting some sort of varmint that was attacking the Darleys' chickens. They also went on hikes up the wooded hill, took the kids down to the pond in the valley below, and inspected the animal pens. Our kids played a good bit of the time outside with the Darley kids, while Jeanetta and I worked on stitching projects in the warm house, trekking outside to visit the goats on occasion. It was the loveliest, most bucolic weekend, reminding Nathan and me of Phyllis's words from all those years ago.

Finally, the little bit of snow melted and we headed home, back to school and work and life as we knew it. Driving home, sun shining through the windshield, Nathan turned to me and said, "I know what I want to do. I want to live like that."

It is now a well-known truth that if you give a mouse a cookie he will ask for a glass of milk, and just as true is that if you tell me what will make you happy, I will immediately do everything in my power to make it happen. Especially if that thing is a desire that has lain dormant in my soul for years. Within a few short weeks of Nathan's proclamation, I had found a house for sale with twenty acres, within driving distance from our work and schools, and within our price range.

I had found the solution and formulated a plan. We would sell our house, move to the small farm, and Nathan, and our family, would be happy. I would have my heart's desire—a happy husband and a happy home—and I would no longer be desperate. We would finally raise our boys on the land before it was too late. Things would be lovely. And I was all in. I had never wanted anything as much as I wanted that farm, that life, that happiness. We just had to follow the plan.

chapter 3

Running

To put the world right in order, we must first put the
nation in order; to put the nation in order, we must
first put the family in order; to put the family in order,
we must first cultivate our personal life; we must first
set our hearts right.
—Confucius

The first part of our plan to leave our messy life and start fresh was to sell our
house. There was no way we could afford two mortgages, and we had no desire to
be landlords, so the obvious solution was to list the house and hope it sold fast.
The day before the For Sale sign went up in our yard, I scrubbed the floors, dusted
the shelves, fluffed the pillows, and made the beds. Confident that our cute 1940s
cottage in a historic neighborhood would sell quickly, I tweeted my excitement out
to the world and began a Pinterest board for the Farm House. Surely it would only
be a matter of days, maybe a few weeks at most, before we had an offer. Our house
had been featured in magazines such as *Flea Market Style* and *At Home in Arkansas*,
and was full of character and charm; it was instantly lovable. All I needed to do was
wait patiently and keep the house clean.

I have this thing for rescuing junk from the side of the road, the back of dimly lit thrift stores, and my friend's divorces or moves. I have written about it before. My attraction to what others have thrown away or what others fail to see the beauty in applies to dogs and children and furniture, lamps and causes and books. I want to adopt all the orphans and abandoned dogs and buy all the quilts that have too many stains and holes in them to be considered valuable. It is only Nathan Greer, the Arkansas legal system, and my bank account that keep me from doing these things daily. My love of quirky, colorful items—mismatched thrift-store furniture, vintage textiles, and reclaimed items such as chalkboards, screen windows, and typewriters—has always been part of my decorating style. My style also includes a love of bright, cheerful hues that goes deep and wide. In fact, it goes all over the walls. Our first house had walls the color of snow peas and with a kitchen the color of a jewelry box from Tiffany's. This house, the 1940s cottage, had a pinky-red dining room and a two-tone kitchen with green cabinets and warm Tuscan yellow walls. The bathroom was map blue, the front door was fire engine red, and the patio walls were hot pink. The living room was a cool aqua and the boys' room two shades of kelly green. The house was photographed for both local and national magazines. Pictures of our red dining room with the aqua table and lime bench are so frequently pinned and repinned on Pinterest that I stumble across them weekly quite by accident.

But despite the magazine spreads, the Pinterest success, and sweet comments from Instagram followers, once the For Sale sign went in the yard we quickly discovered that the real-life version of our house was not nearly as loved by the house-hunting population as it had been by the online population. Apparently a house that looks like the inside of an Easter egg diorama is not what most people are looking for in a new home. Instead, people were looking for neutral palettes and they could afford to be choosey, which they let us know with every comment our agent forwarded us post-showing. Can I just tell you how much I loathed those forms? They are the worst. Every time one showed up in my inbox I felt as if I was in junior high all over again, where any and everything that made you different was magnified and ridiculed. Just like the popular girl commenting on your generic sneakers, or the boy in P. E. mocking your inability to run fast, each and every picky comment that came in made me feel small. The complaints covered all manner of house-selling sins: the paint colors too bright, the kitchen too mismatched and dated, the roof too old, the exterior paint too flaky, the bathrooms too few, the landscaping too nonexistent. Finally, we asked our Realtor to please never, ever show us another post-showing comment. My blood pressure and my ego couldn't take any more criticism.

Still, we wanted to sell the house, and even though we didn't like the negative critiques, we had heard what the potential buyers were saying, so Nathan and I decided to make a few cosmetic changes to both the interior and exterior of the house hoping to gain some new interest. But my heart wasn't in this plan at all, and when I say we worked to make improvements, you should understand that what I mean is that we did the bare minimum; specifically, I did the bare minimum, to update and improve the house. Instead of being filled with motivation, humility, and honesty, I was instead filled with resentment, petulance, and selfishness. Instead of investing real money into this house, I wanted to save every penny we could to fix up our someday-farmhouse. I didn't want to invest in a new roof, or spend what it would take to update the kitchen or gut the bathroom. I wanted to do those things in my new house, not my old, crummy one. In other words, I wanted what I wanted, and I didn't want to sacrifice a thing to get it.

So I chose the easiest route (because I really did want to sell the house, I just didn't want to spend anything) and decided to neutralize our rainbow-colored cottage. I sent Nathan to the store for gallons of pale-hued paint, found Huey Lewis and the News' album *Fore* on Spotify and turned the volume way up. This began the exorcism of color. I painted my beautiful two-toned green kitchen cabinets country white, next covering the Tuscan yellow walls with a barely-there-aqua. I erased my beautiful red dining room with a polar ice white. Using a half-empty can from a salvage store and several leftover sample pints of various shades of cool green, I painted over the lovely ocean-blue of our bathroom walls. (With the used can and samples, I didn't have enough to properly cover the walls, and anyone who looked close enough could see thin places where the old rich blue—the color of every ocean on every school room globe—peeked through. Later, I found I avoided looking in the direction of those thin places, where the wisps of blue paint staring back at me mocked my so-called efforts to Do What Was Needed to sell the house. "You are a liar and a fraud," they would say. "This house isn't worth selling; you have done a lousy job taking care of it. If people only knew what is really behind those pictures in the magazines. You are a fake. And now you are acting like some martyr because your house won't sell. You are an emperor with no clothes on."

Those walls, they knew the truth and the truth was this: I hadn't done all of what was needed to prepare our house to sell and I had never intended to. I wanted the house to sell, yes. I just didn't want to have to give up anything in order for that to happen. I didn't want to sacrifice, or sweat, or change, or grow, or bend my will to the buyers' wants. I was as stiff as an old paintbrush that had been left out to dry, still coated with paint. I saw no reason to invest in something I was just going to leave soon, so I did what I accuse my children of doing all the time when it comes to their chores. I did the bare minimum that I could get away with and still claim I had made an effort. I did just enough to be able to raise my shoulders and feign bewilderment when people asked why I thought the house wasn't selling. I did just enough work that I could look at God and say, "See, I did my part, now show up, would ya?" And yet I knew it was all a false front. I knew the game I was playing, as would anyone who stared at my bathroom walls long enough.

Before things went south for good, there was a day I treated myself to a deluxe package pedicure. I paid my hard-earned money for the full pampering treatment, and after many repetitions of hot wax, hotter water, and lots of hard scrubbing, my feet looked ten times better than any other part of me. From the ankles down, my skin positively glowed; from the ankles up, however, I was tattered, worn, and droopy, and covered with paint flakes.

The hours leading up to the pedicure had been spent scraping the seventy-five-year-old windows on the outside of our house. Scraping windows is one of those chores that can only be done slowly. Repeatedly. Diligently. Painstakingly. There are no good shortcuts. And it is awful, boring, sweat-producing, tedious work. I was scraping our windows so that we could repaint them a newer, shinier, more appealing hue of white, in an attempt to lure a buyer for our house. I was scraping them because I was desperate. I was ready to move, and it was just not happening, so there I was, outside, in the blazing sun, pushing and scraping our ancient, peeling windows.

In an attempt to entice Jesus to show me favor and sell this damn house for me, I prayed while I scraped. I thanked him for our house. For the windows and the flaky paint and the beautiful day to scrape them. I thanked him for our friends who had come to help with scraping the eighteen windows, some of which were floor to ceiling. I thanked him that we even had a house, let alone one with big, beautiful old windows, old hardwood floors and central heat and air. While I prayed I tried really hard not to think about how I had hoped these windows would be someone else's problem by now, about how what I really wanted to be thanking God for was a new house and twenty acres. But it was no use.

Both Jesus and I could see straight through my flimsy tissue-paper-heart prayers. I was an ungrateful fraud and we both knew it. So I gave up. I stopped praying, stopped scraping and peeling, and went inside, where I was greeted by all the other projects and rooms in the house still waiting to be repaired, finished, and cleaned. The living room ceiling that needed patching, the scarred wood floors, the half-painted dining room, the overflowing laundry, and the ancient, mismatched kitchen appliances. They all were all openly mocking me. There was only one thing to do. Flee the scene.

I grabbed a stack of books and headed straight for the day spa, where I hoped to rid myself of both ugly toenail polish and a bad attitude. While I sat with my feet in plastic bags filled with hot wax, I switched between reading The Rule of St. Benedict and reading about The Rule in Dennis Okholm's *Monk Habits for Everyday People: Benedictine Spirituality for Protestants*. I was busily highlighting away like a good student, when I stumbled over these words: "Conversion and growth in character happen when we remain, not when we run. . . . Stability means being faithful where we are—really paying attention to those with whom we live and to what is happening in our common life." At that moment, these words were the exact opposite of what I wanted to hear, but I could not move on. I was arrested. I read those words again and again, letting their weight, their caution, and their guidance soak into my heart just the tiniest bit as the hot wax was soaking into my skin.

Staying put in our current home was not a bad life. It was actually a very lovely life in a lot of ways. The kids had a good school, our mortgage was manageable, we lived near friends; our house, while tattered around the edges, was adorable, and the dark cloud over Nathan had begun to shrink. I knew all of these facts in the same part of my brain where I make decisions to pay the light bill, take a shower, and drive on the right side of the road. They were the logical, rational responses to my ungrateful whining. But it was the other part of my brain that was making all the ruckus, the all-emotion and feelings and desires part. The part that stomps its feet, clenches its fists tightly, and screams, "This is not what I want!"

In *Acedia and Me*, Kathleen Norris wrote: "We want life to have meaning, and want to be fulfilled, and it is hard to accept that we find these things by starting where we are, not where we would like to be. Our greatest spiritual blessings are likely to reveal themselves not in exotic settings but in everyday tasks and trials."

I had decided I needed, I wanted, I had to have, that house and those twenty acres. It was *the thing* that would fix *everything*, and I wanted it yesterday. Sitting there in the pedicure chair, reading those words of Dennis Okholm's over and over, I began to realize I had painted myself into a petulant corner and it was sucking all the joy out of my life.

And yet I was determined. So I marched forward, pushing, cajoling, fighting, and ignoring what now seems painfully obvious: we weren't ready.

chapter 4

Falling

No one escapes the wilderness on the way to the Promised Land.
—Annie Dillard

Hip deep in trying to finish edits and photo shoots for my book *A Homemade Year*, as well as trying to keep our house and yard presentable for showings, I was already running on empty when, in March, our precious, ancient family dog passed away. The day Nathan drove her to the vet for the last time, I lay on the swing in our backyard, tears and snot puddling under my cheek. The boys had both retreated inside to mourn privately in their own ways, and before long eight-year-old Miles came outside and handed me a ham sandwich, bringing food being the best way he knew to offer solace.

Two weeks after Chloe passed away, we woke to find our six backyard hens had been killed by a vicious owl attack in the middle of the night. Wylie had gone outside to feed them, and I will never forget the guttural wail of grief I heard as he discovered their headless carcasses tossed all around the backyard. That morning, standing in the middle of the carnage, a cloud of dense fog surrounding our entire property, my heart broken by our loss and Wylie's deep anguish, I wept and wept as Nathan held me, saying over and over, "It's just too much. It's just too much."

A small glimmer of hope would shine on Easter weekend when we received and accepted an offer on our house, but even that was too good to be true. The buyer's demands increased week after week, and wanting so desperately to move, we conceded one after another. But it didn't matter. In the end they withdrew their offer one week before the closing date, leaving us with a half-packed house and busted plans.

Completely deflated and desperate for a change in scenery, we packed up the car and went on a weeklong family vacation. Somewhere in the middle of camping and sightseeing and ice cream cones, I told Nathan we needed an end date. I needed a finish line to all of this striving. So we set a date and made a deal. If the house didn't sell by the end of the summer we would take it off the market and resign ourselves to staying put for the foreseeable future. Which is exactly what happened.

I endeavor to have faith and a tranquil, patient demeanor. I aspire to be filled with contentment, loving as Christ loves, selfless and wise. When I am in a healthy, whole, smooth-going place, these seem like reasonable attributes. They seem doable—at least four out of seven days. But when I am disappointed, worn out, frustrated, and fear-filled, I turn into an impatient, whiny, cursing, short-tempered, irrational, selfish soul who desperately wants to know the secret password that will convince God to give me what I want. When we took our house off the market and let our offer on the farm expire, I put on a brave face, but I was heartbroken and angry. Being an optimistic-Pollyanna type, I don't do angry well. It is not my first language. Sadness is the verbiage I know best. So I took to my bed like some grand Southern diva, and cried big hot tears, ate a lot of ice cream, and watched a lot of *The Real Housewives*. When I finally got out of bed, I discovered I could not ignore my anger. I was mad. Really, really, mad. At God, the universe, the buyers, the owls, my husband, myself . . . you name it.

So I took all my anger and disappointment and I ran straight into the Land of Denial, all the while giving lip service to this new plan, working overtime to find the bright spots in why staying really was for the best, blogging about all the fun changes I would make to the house now since the pressure to sell was behind me. But it was all lies and it was all running.

I ran so fast and so hard during this season that I fell and broke my right foot in three places. It was on a Wednesday night, one week before Halloween. Nathan was downtown playing music at a local restaurant and I was home trying to get the boys ready for bed and the house straightened enough for our occasional housecleaning lady. In my rush to do twenty things at once, tired after an already-long work day, I knocked over a seven-foot-long, solid wood bench, breaking its fall with my bare right foot.

Jonah had his big life-changing aha moment in the belly of a fish and Saul had his on the road to Damascus. Me? Mine happened on a sectional sofa. I know what you are thinking: how very American. And you would be right. I would have much preferred an ancient cathedral in Europe, or the cliffs of Dover or, at the very least, walking through a field of sunflowers. But nope. I got a sofa. A sixty-dollar, second-hand sofa. In the long run, though, it really does suit this whole story better, and maybe it is proof enough that God is somehow at work in my life.

chapter 5

Sitting

You do not need to know precisely what is happening, or exactly where it is all going. What you need is to recognize the possibilities and challenges offered by the present moment, and to embrace them with courage, faith and hope.
—Thomas Merton

Now instead of running, there would only be sitting. Sitting with myself and all that had built up inside my heart over the past months: blame, anger, fear, sadness, disappointment. Did I mention anger? Apparently, you can't starve bitterness by ignoring it. As it turns out, ignoring these emotions and truths only makes them grow deeper, latch on tighter, as they feast on rich and juicy denial. Sentenced to the couch, foot propped up, nowhere left to run, I had no way to pretend to be happy or settled with the way things had turned out. As I cried more big-diva-style, heaving tears over the fact that I would not be cutting down my Christmas tree on my own farm, I realized nothing was going to get better as long as I held on to wanting to be somewhere other than where I was.

I do not believe in formulas when it comes to faith. I do not believe that if I do *this*, then God must do *that*. But I do believe in the power and gift of the Scriptures and in the wisdom within them. I recently heard the very wise Episcopalian priest Carol Mead say, "Often the Bible tells us a truth, by way of a story, one we would have too hard a time hearing or seeing if our best friend or spouse told us." Some people find truth and freedom through the story of Jonah or the Prodigal Son or Paul's conversion. I found mine in Jeremiah, of all places.

Now, I am not sure if this is true of Christians all over the world, but in the South, where I live, Christians love platitudes. And we like to plaster them over anything that will stand still. And one of the well-loved platitudes we print like a monogram in cute calligraphy on pillows and tote bags is Jeremiah 29:11: "'For I know the plans I have for you,' declares the LORD, 'plans to prosper you and not to harm you, plans to give you hope and a future'" (NIV).

You probably know this verse. Someone might have even posted a cute Instagram picture of it this morning. Does this verse drive anyone else batty? Just like completely nuts? Because it drives me mad. Somehow, somewhere, we have gotten the idea that these are comforting words. Reassuring words. "God's got the whole world in his hands" sort of words. But to someone experiencing pain and loss, these words smack of mockery and abandonment.

When the Year of All the Awful Things happened, this verse was quoted to me over and over. And I was not taking it well. In fact it had gotten to the point that if one more person told me God had a plan in all of this, I might lose my cool all over their Facebook wall. To me, Jeremiah's words felt like a hollow promise and a sales gimmick. The fervor with which people claimed them as a battle cry seemed to suggest they were using the words to stave off disappointment, fear of the unknown and disillusionment with the way their lives were going.

I felt I could say with confidence that this broken foot business was not a great plan. Certainly not a plan for a future and a hope. Furthermore, all the sitting provided ample opportunities to think back to all the other recent missed opportunities for a great future. *Where are these great plans?* I wondered as I thought back to the previous spring when the sale of our house tanked days before closing. Where is this prospering? I wondered as I watched the farm we had set our hopes on slip from our grasp.

And "not to harm you"? What about my foot broken in three places? I can tell you, it hurt. And our flock of chickens brutally killed during a midnight owl raid? Or our family dog of eleven years that died just a few months ago? Plenty of harm had been done. And "give you hope"? Where was that? I was supposed to be celebrating Christmas on the farm, trotting around on two good feet, not here, in the same old house, on the couch with a broken foot.

But not wanting to completely give over to cynicism, and believing *surely* there was more to Jeremiah 29 than this one infuriating verse, I did what I do when I cannot take a certain passage or verse being thrown in my face repeatedly with no context. I broke out my Bible (or maybe I broke out BibleGateway.com) and I looked up Jeremiah 29. In whole.

And I was a bit flummoxed.

Well, first I was excited. And then I was flummoxed. And then excited again.

Because I read the whole dadgum thing. Not just the pretty verse, but the rest of it. The rest of it is good. It is meat. It makes sense. It feels real, and authentic, and messy, and still a little elusive, but in a life-is-just-like-that way. Not in a follow-the-carrot-of-false-hope sort of way.

Here is what I found in the verses surrounding verse 11:

This is the Message from GOD-of-the-Angel-Armies, Israel's God, to all the exiles I've taken from Jerusalem to Babylon:

"Build houses and make yourselves at home.

"Put in gardens and eat what grows in that country.

"Marry and have children. Encourage your children to marry and have children so that you'll thrive in that country and not waste away.

"Make yourselves at home there and work for the country's welfare.

"Pray for Babylon's well-being. If things go well for Babylon, things will go well for you."

Yes. Believe it or not, this is the Message from GOD-of-the-Angel-Armies, Israel's God: "Don't let all those so-called preachers and know-it-alls who are all over the place there take you in with their lies. Don't pay any attention to the fantasies they keep coming up with to please you. They're a bunch of liars preaching lies—and claiming I sent them! I never sent them, believe me." GOD's Decree!

This is GOD's Word on the subject: "As soon as Babylon's seventy years are up and not a day before, I'll show up and take care of you as I promised and bring you back home. I know what I'm doing. I have it all planned out—plans to take care of you, not abandon you, plans to give you the future you hope for.

"When you call on me, when you come and pray to me, I'll listen.

"When you come looking for me, you'll find me.

"Yes, when you get serious about finding me and want it more than anything else, I'll make sure you won't be disappointed." GOD's Decree.

"I'll turn things around for you. I'll bring you back from all the countries into which I drove you"—GOD's Decree—"bring you home to the place from which I sent you off into exile. You can count on it." (Jer. 29:4–14 MSG)

And this is what these verses said to me:

This is where you are. Best settle in for a bit.

Build houses.

Plant a garden.

Get married.

Raise your kids.

Have grandkids.

Work for peace in your community.

Work for your community's prosperity.

Pray for your community.

Don't listen to motivational speakers or model your life after reality television.

Do not be tricked into thinking you need/deserve/have to have more.

(Oh, wait, it doesn't actually say that. But it does say to not be tricked by so-called prophets, fortune-tellers, and false preachers. Close enough?)

Settle here. This is home for a while.

Don't worry—I've got this.

I have given you a plan for your immediate future, and it is a plan full of hope.

So keep talking to me. I am listening.

If you need me, look for me. I am here.

You can always find me.

Eventually things will change.

But for now, settle in.

This is home.

Sitting on my couch, foot in cast, holiday and life plans completely jacked up, I had my very own conversion experience. But instead of hearing God say, "Go," I heard him say, very clearly, "Stay." Which brought both peace and panic inside my heart.

I had counted on our "going"—moving to the farm and thus changing our life through circumstances—to be the ointment that would soothe my over-stressed, over-scheduled, over-anxious life. I had counted on moving to make me happy. To make my husband happy. To be a new adventure to distract us from all that was broken in our lives. Sitting in a house I had come to have so little regard for, for months on end, with all of our problems piling up around me during the holiday season was not my idea of adventure. And yet, I found comfort in the words of Jeremiah 29. Something about the simplicity of God's directions to the Israelites living in a place not of their choosing settled in my heart and sprouted the tiniest bit of hope.

And interestingly, I noticed how these verses, including the ones that follow them, reminded me a whole lot of the Rule of St. Benedict, a plan for living a balanced, simple, and prayerful life in the context of community, written by the fifth-century monk St. Benedict of Nursia. The Rule's primary teachings center around these vows: stability—God will work in us when we choose to remain where we have been planted, through both the people and the geographical location; conversion—we must continually grow and change, allowing the Holy Spirit to work within us; and obedience—we place Christ and not ourselves at the centers of our lives, thereby learning to love and serve as he loved and served. Jeremiah 29 echoes these same ideas. *Make yourselves at home here* (Stability), w*ork and pray for the good of Babylon* (Conversion), *and keep looking for me, I am here* (Obedience).

As I sat on my couch for months on end, foot in boot, heart in throat, I thought a lot about Jeremiah 29, and how verses 4 through 14 intersected with the teachings of St. Benedict, how together they seemed both radical and obvious. They were to me a mystical combination. A combination that inspired hope in me that I could find a way to be present to my life, as it was, without throwing out my dreams and desires with the bathwater.

Reading Jeremiah confirmed a suspicion that had begun with reading St. Benedict: balance isn't a matter of getting what we think will make us happy; it is about cultivating a grateful and present heart right where we are.

This realization led to these questions:

What if, instead of seeking balance, I seek rootedness?

Can I find a way to live a slower version of modern life?

Is it possible to slow down, internally, right where I am, without changing my external circumstances—jobs, schools, home, or responsibilities?

Can our family find a way to use the passage from Jeremiah as a scaffolding to help us rebuild the way we live, to do as God instructs through the words of Jeremiah: to put down roots, to plant a garden, to embrace and serve our community, to stop worshiping the greener grass, throw out the pursuit of balance, and instead dig in where we are with gratefulness, no matter our circumstances?

Would this reorientation of our hearts help create a simpler and more sustainable life from the inside out?

Can we grow deep spiritual roots producing fruit in our day-to-day lives?

I didn't know, but I was certainly willing to try. As soon as my boot came off, we were going to find out.

PART 2

STAYING

And don't be wishing you were someplace
else or with someone else.
Where you are right now is God's place for
you. Live and obey and love and believe
right there.

—1 Corinthians 7:17 (MSG)

chapter 6

Stability, Stewardship, and Painting Walls

To make old paint brushes pliable, heat in hot linseed
oil and work the bristles back and forth.
—*Short-Cuts to Home Making* (1952)

I can practice my faith in all the places that I don't
want to be, in the middle of the mess of it all. When
there is cheer and warmth, or when I'm rusty, tired,
dirty, fat. I can show up, and I can sing. And his grace
will be enough even for me.
—Sarabeth Jones, January 6, 2015, on her blog *The
Dramatic,* in the post "Sing Yourself In."

When spring arrived, I had been out of the boot for a few months, and had begun
to walk normally, albeit gingerly, again. I had also generally made my peace with
staying put. And by generally, I mean I had given up the fantasies where someone

was going to knock on our door and offer to buy our house because it was just so charming. Also the farm had sold to someone else. That ship had sailed. Logically, in the part of my brain where I know bills must be paid and a diet of only cookies and French fries will kill me, I knew that if I were going to commit to following St. Benedict's teachings, if I were going to try the experiment of putting into action the verses of Jeremiah 29, specifically verse 4—to make myself at home in this life— then I was going to have to learn to care for our house again.

Build houses and make yourselves at home there is one of the very first directions that God gives the Israelites in Jeremiah 29, and this was the one I got stuck on time and time again. I had tried to build (okay, buy) a house in the country, failed disastrously, and was still a little bitter about it. But if I was going to learn how to make myself at home in this life—if I was really going to dig in and learn how to slow down—I was going to have to bring the principles of St. Benedict's Rule home.

Stability is one of the key vows of Benedictine monasticism. Stability comes from the Latin word *stabilis*, which means to stand, to be still, to stand firm, to be rooted. When a Benedictine monk takes this vow, he is committing to both the people and the geography of a certain place, believing it is through both that God will do a good work in him.

As someone who was having a hard time embracing the idea of "staying put," the idea that God could use my physical location—especially a location I resisted—to inspire change within me was a crazy notion. As a lifelong Christian I knew plenty about being changed in the context of relationships, iron against iron, river over stones, and so forth and so on. But up until now I had never considered how God could work through—perhaps even desired to work through—my relationship with a physical place, geographical location, four walls, and a Zip Code.

As I read about this vow, as I thought about how I could "remain steadfast and faithful to the situation" where I found myself, I realized that in order to really practice the spiritual discipline of stability, I was going to have to open myself up and do my best to settle in right where I was. I was going to have to love and care for the house I had instead of the house I wanted. I was going to have tend to her, mend her, and treasure her. And I was also going to have to forgive myself for all the neglect I had subjected her to in the first place.

It will not come as a shock that despite these heroic (I use that term ever so loosely) efforts of mine to neutralize the interior and half of the exterior, our house still didn't sell. We received one offer, but the buyers pulled out a week before closing because of all the problems the inspection found. It wasn't just paint colors and countertops that needed updating. There was so much more underneath, problems we had ignored for years. When the house didn't sell I was so angry. I was angry at the buyers who backed out, I was angry at everyone who hadn't liked my Easter-egg house, and I was angry with myself. By the time I got out of The Boot, I was worn smooth out from all the anger. I decided to begin again, start fresh, doing my best to build a house here and make myself at home once again.

And I did. Sort of. In the beginning my efforts were the type that come from a change of mind but not quite a change of heart. While I believed in my mind that cultivating an attitude of steadfastness was a God-led way to live, the reality of taking the actions needed was daunting. To me, our entire situation was overwhelming, the list of things to be done too long, and the payoff unclear. But I forged on, hoping I could fake it till I could make it, gambling on the chance that if I pretended to be excited about once again putting my stamp on the house, I would catch the nest-fluffing fever.

The first thing I did was beg my mother to come hang some paintable wallpaper for me in the dining room. I had found vintage paintable wallpaper on Craigslist for a steal and I was determined to use it somewhere in our house. Once the wallpaper was hung, my plan was to paint it a very striking color of mustard. I was determined to take back my design aesthetic with a vengeance. "No more boring white walls for me!" I thought.

So my mother hung the wallpaper and I bought the paint. And this is as far as I got. Paper on the walls. Paint in the can. Unfinished. So much for my battle cry against the generic white walls. "It is not perfection that leads us to God: it is perseverance," writes Sr. Joan Chittister, but I was barely making an effort to persevere.

After the dining room "update" I moved on to the kitchen. I painted the new-to-me kitchen bar stools in our little breakfast nook. I hung new curtains, changed the hardware on the cabinets, put up new artwork, painted a light fixture, and called it a day. It was all the nest fluffing I could muster.

Around this time my first book had come out and I was busy trying to promote and launch it into the world. Whatever creative, passionate energy I had was funneled in that direction, and I spent a good chunk of the spring traveling to events and conferences from one end of the promotion spectrum to the other, all while trying to maintain the blog, hold down a job, and raise our boys.

While I struggled to find energy and desire to fall back in love with our house and accept our situation with joy, Nathan struggled with his own desire to care for our home on a practical level. As winter approached, our house was invaded by rats. Hideous, disgusting, monstrous rats. The kind of rats that belong in the back alleys of New York City, the kind of rats that give grown men nightmares with their hissing and spitting and scampering out from dark corners. During the Great Rat Invasion, the ungodly beasts killed our dishwasher, our washing machine, and stunk up the laundry room and kitchen. They chewed through Rubbermaid bins in the attic, strewing Easter grass and Christmas tinsel everywhere. Places we had left unchecked in our neglect had become perfect entry points all around our house for these beasts. Rotted places in the roof line of our back patio, rotted floor boards under our kitchen sink and dishwasher cabinets, places where there had been water leaks and the wood had softened and rotted away—each of these places might as well have had a huge neon sign above it with RATS WELCOME in big, flashing letters.

In previous winters we had seen a critter here or there, but never this onslaught. And what we had managed to contain in the past with small traps and little bits of poison here and there exploded out of control very quickly. Things got so bad that I would not walk from our bedroom to the kitchen, passing through the laundry room, their romper room of fun, between 10 PM and 6 AM without Nathan going ahead of me to check for rats, dead or alive. (I admit it. I am a little freaked out by rats. Even dead ones. Maybe even especially dead ones.) Eventually spring arrived and the war with the rat kings subsided. Nathan was the conquering hero, but we both knew the victory was temporary. Next winter they would be back with a vengeance if something wasn't done.

Spring turned into summer, and I tried once more to jolly myself into caring for our home. We planted a small garden, we raised our new chickens, we set out the big blow-up pool I had enjoyed so much the summer before. But the garden was eaten up by opportunistic rabbits, birds, and worms. The summer was full of rain and busier than the year before with more book-related travel, so the pool sat full of dirty rainwater and tree leaves most days. The exterior of the house wasn't faring much better. It was still green on the front and white on the back, and only half of the windows had been re-glazed and painted. Everywhere I looked things were in a state of half-doneness. Nothing was finished, nothing was whole, and I couldn't seem to muster much interest in caring if it ever would be.

Then our ceiling fell in and all hell broke loose. Well, that might be a tad dramatic. The whole thing didn't fall, just a portion of it in the living room. And all hell didn't really break loose, but I felt as if it might as I teetered on the edge between holding it together and losing my mind.

Dormers succumbed to a season of unrelenting rain, bringing the lovely summer showers indoors. Nathan patched the holes on the roof and then the ceiling, but, much like the rat problem, we knew this was not a permanent solution. Things were not getting much better despite our tepid attempts at practicing the vow of Stability, they might be getting worse, and there was no sign of relief in sight—no get-out-of-jail-free card, no change that would relieve us of our responsibilities to this place. This little patch of land and this house we called home were where God had planted us, and there was no escape hatch. We had played those cards and lost.

To add insult to injury, every time something broke or went belly up, all I could think about was the critical feedback forms buyers had written about our house while it was for sale. They had seen all the things we had tried to ignore or hide; they had seen through more than just my thinly painted walls. I felt as if someone had ripped the big green velvet curtain of Oz back, exposing our magazine-photographed house for what it really was: a crumbly mess. Buyers saw not the cute, thrifty, vintage home I had shown on my blog, but flaking paint, rotten kitchen cabinet floors, a sagging window unit, clogged plumbing, and a horribly decrepit old roof. I began to see our house through their eyes and I was mortified. I felt as if I had been rejected, exposed as a fraud, naked and unaware.

One of the themes woven into Benedictine living is humility. St. Benedict teaches what is perhaps the original Twelve-Step Program—twelve steps to achieving a humble spirit. Without humility (a virtue rooted in love), he says, the quest to live out the vows of Stability, Conversion, and Obedience will be frustrating, futile, and filled with vanity. Sr. Joan Chittister sums it up this way: "Benedict wants us to realize that accepting our essential smallness and embracing it frees us from the need to lie, even to ourselves, about our frailties."

My attempts to start fresh, re-fluffing my nest and trying to make myself at home right where I was instead of where I wanted to be, had failed because I had continued to lie to myself about my frailties. I had run from my smallness instead of embracing it. I had avoided my limitations instead of laying them bare before God and myself, facing the truth of what I had and had not done. I had smacked lipstick on a pig and called it beautiful.

In September, Nathan and I slipped away for a weekend in a cabin at a nearby state park. We went away to celebrate our birthdays (which are only two days apart) and to take stock of our lives and our situation, and to see if we could tease out some sort of clarity about how to proceed in the face of all our problems. The time had come to be grown-ups: we had grieved and used temporary fixes long enough. We needed to stop being afraid we would be consumed by everything that was wrong with our house and our lives. We needed to persevere through the darkest of our fears until we made it through to the other side, into the light, where hope and a plan would surely emerge. Plus, winter was fast approaching, bringing more rain and more rats. Now was the time to take serious action; no more Band-Aids, no more lipstick.

Sitting in a small fishing skiff on a beautiful lake, surrounded by trees just beginning to take on their autumn glow, the sunlight bouncing off the water, Nathan fished, and I read aloud portions of the book *Free* by Mark and Lisa Scandrette. I had met Mark and Lisa at the Wild Goose Festival when we were all promoting our various books. *Free* is a book about learning to spend your time and money on what matters most to you. Hearing Mark and Lisa speak at the festival had sparked a hope in me that somehow Nathan and I could figure out how to be better stewards of all we had been given. I found their attitude and their approach refreshing, authentic, and helpful, and remarkably in line with both my rooting passages in Jeremiah and the vows of St. Benedict.

Puttering around the lake, we discussed some of the questions Mark and Lisa asked. We talked about what was working well and what wasn't. About what we felt God saying to us individually and together. We got honest and shared our fears— even our fears about each other going forward. We talked about our kids, about the sort of values we wanted to live out as a family, and we shared our dreams—realistic and fantastic. We took our heads out of the sand, shook off all the blame we felt toward each other, and honestly addressed the hurdles we saw ahead of us if we were to try and live out those dreams. I will always believe that those few hours paddling around the lake, fishing, eating cheese and salami, and talking changed the trajectory of our life together. That day we discovered two things. The first is that while the life each of us wanted was very similar, neither of us was going to reach that life without the other's help, without the other one cheering and supporting. And secondly, we both still felt a calling to someday, eventually—maybe five or ten years down the road—move to the country. To buy a house with some acreage and a pond, a place where we could slow down and dig in—not just metaphorically, but physically as well. A place where we could see the stars and hear ourselves breathe.

But how? How could we begin to live a life that would move us toward our dream, instead of away from it? What could we do then, where we were, to invest in our calling? Ironically, it seemed the only way to move toward the someday was to stop and dig in where we were, addressing the problems of the here-and-now head on. Pragmatically, what was very clear to both of us that weekend was that regardless of whether we were going to stay in our house for another ten years, or whether we would try again to sell it sooner, things could not stay as they were.

We asked ourselves why on earth God would entrust us with more house and more land when we couldn't even take care of what we had. What right did we have to pray for a new life when we were not willing to care for and give thanks for what we already had? This conviction had been growing in us both, and that day, sliding over the lake waters, we could no longer deny what we both knew had to be done. We were going to have to do the big, expensive things to the house we had been putting off for years. Instead of trying to escape the problems by foisting them off on an unsuspecting buyer, we needed to address them. We were going to have to finish painting the house. We were going to have to replace the roof and fix all the rotting wood underneath the kitchen and laundry room. We were going to have to gut the bathroom and update the kitchen. We were going to have to repaint the living room, filling in the hundred-plus nail holes I had made over the years as I decorated and redecorated.

This was our home, even if it wasn't the one we wanted, and we believed part of our call was to be good stewards of it. We knew in our gut that to persevere in caring for it—even in the face of what seemed to be an insurmountable list of chores and projects—was one way we could live out the vow of Stability we'd made to each other and to God: making ourselves at home, right where we were.

Perseverance is not something St. Benedict talks about directly in his Rule, but it is a thread that is woven throughout all the pages, especially in the passages on humility. John McQuiston II interprets St. Benedict's fourth stage of humility this way:

> The fourth stage of humility is to be patient even in the face of inequity, injury, and contradiction, preserving the awareness that we are ever shaped by experience and refined by fire, and accordingly to be thankful even for the injuries.

I am fairly certain that when St. Benedict wrote of injury and refining fire he wasn't talking about the injury to the ego that occurs when you know you have given your house over to the Rat King, or the refining fire of your roof caving in; however,

I found the gift of humility in them, learning—however slowly and stubbornly. To give thanks for these injuries, these humiliating lessons, was to learn from them, and to do all I could to heal them.

When we got home from our weekend on the lake, Nathan called the bank and I called a roofing company. We were both afraid and nervous to step out on this limb and to use our savings and incur more debt (something we try to avoid) toward repairing the house, but we knew we could no longer stand around, wringing our hands, hoping things would somehow get better on their own. We knew the time had come to sing a new song in faith. Or as *The Message* renders Psalm 100:2, sing ourselves into his presence. But instead of words and a melody, we would be singing with our obedience, our paint brushes, our hammers, and our spackle.

A Few Words about Painting Walls

Don't ever pick the paint color in the store. Ever. Trust me. This is a disaster.

Go to your favorite paint store and take all the little paint chips home that you even remotely like.

Tape them all on the wall of the room you are going to paint.

Stare at them for a while.

Narrow it down to your favorite two or three. If you can afford it, go buy those little sample cans of each of those two or three colors.

Paint a swatch of each color on your wall.

Look at the paint after it dries in every sort of light: in the daylight, at night with the overhead lights on, in the evening with lamps on, with the curtains open and the curtains closed.

The one you like best no matter the lighting—that is your color.

Fill all the nail holes in with filler. Even the tiny ones.

Prime your walls. Please. The color underneath will change the color you have picked out if you don't. Unless your walls are white to begin with. If this is the case, then you are very lucky.

The quality of the brush or roller always matters.

The quality of the paint sometimes matters. I buy my white paint right off the shelf at a big-box store. It is a premixed color and it has never let me down.

For rich colors, I pay extra and go to the paint store (but I always use coupons). The thicker the paint the better it covers.

Remember, the finish will change the color a bit. Try to go with satin or eggshell if you have kids—it cleans up so much easier than flat.

The ceiling color and the floor color will impact the wall color. If you are changing those things, you might want to wait and choose your paint after they are completed, or at the very least, with them in mind.

chapter 7

Simplicity, Fasting, and Laundry

To whiten your linens, let them soak in buttermilk for twenty-four hours; then rinse in cool water and finally in tepid water.
—*Short-Cuts to Home Making*

Benedict is splendidly precise. Everything matters, down to the last detail. There is such loving and careful respect and care for clothes in the way they are to be washed and stored after use.
—Esther De Waal

Some families talk about the weather, some talk about politics, some talk about sports. In our family, we talk about the laundry. Case in point: my ninety-one-year-old grandmother recently lamented about how her favorite detergent formula is no longer working up to her standards, and she can't figure out why. In fact she was losing a bit of sleep over the matter until we discovered she had mistakenly purchased one of those newfangled, energy-efficient formulas meant for the newfangled, energy-efficient machines. But not to worry, we got Maw her old-fashioned detergent for her old-fashioned machine, and all is right with her laundry again.

My mother is the all-time world champion laundry goddess. Tanya Beverly Jackson can get stains out of anything, and no one can get clothes as clean, smelling as fresh, or feeling as soft. If you snoop in my parents' laundry room cabinets you will discover they are as stocked full as any small-town pharmacy with potions, powders, sprays, and her own concoctions. My mother is a legendary tightwad, but even she will tell you that if there is one thing she splurges her pennies on, it is her laundry supplies.

My brother Joshua taught us all how to use tennis balls in socks as fabric softener au natural, and my sister Jemimah, a crunchy sort, makes her detergents and softeners from scratch. There is a great and ongoing debate in the family about whether her homemade blend is as good as the store bought, and as you can probably guess, my mother isn't buying what Jemimah is selling.

I am not quite the laundry savant my mother or sister is, but I try to keep up. I have even gone as far as purchasing all the ingredients to make my own detergent, and they sit happily in the top of my laundry cabinet, waiting for inspiration to strike. I want the boys to help me make the detergent, thinking it will be somewhere between a science lesson and an example of frugality and stewardship. "See," I would say as we melted the grated soap over the stove, "we are not being wasteful because we can get three times as many loads cleaned with this as we would with store-bought detergent!" In my daydream they find this to be amazing and life changing, and from then on they argue over who gets to melt the soap when it comes time to make a new batch. In reality, I will probably give all the supplies to Jemimah and ask her to make it for me.

In the family of six I grew up in, there was always laundry. Some of my earliest memories are of hiding in the little laundry hamper closet of my family's Memphis apartment during a game of hide-and-seek. The musty smell of all those dirty clothes was both offensive and comforting as I sat in the dark waiting for someone to find me. No matter where our family lived, from Florida to Alaska, there was always laundry piled on a couch, a load spinning in the wash, a basket of folded underwear to put away. There was so much laundry in our house that "doing the laundry" was the first family-sized chore my siblings and I learned. Sure, there were the personal chores such as Clean Your Room and Make Your Bed and Feed the Fish. But those didn't count as real "chores." Those duties were just the natural consequence of being alive. "Chores" were the things one did to help the greater good, things done around the house that benefitted everyone, separate from basic personal responsibilities like putting away one's shoes (a personal responsibility I still struggle with). Chores in the Jackson household included, but were not limited to, vacuuming, emptying and loading the dishwasher, dusting, mopping, sweeping, and laundry. A lot of laundry. As soon as we kids could read well enough to work the washing machine knobs, and had enough muscle or ingenuity to maneuver a full laundry basket, we were called to the front lines of the war on dirty clothes.

Not surprisingly my mother, the laundress supreme, had a system. Once a child reached the age of laundry accountability, they were assigned the duty of washing all the kitchen and bath towels. When hands and coordination had developed sufficiently, a child would be assigned: (1) whites (mostly underwear and T-shirts); (2) knits (the largest loads by far); and (3) pants (not as large as knits but requiring more skill as there was the whole center leg crease to manage). Permanent press was the final rung in the laundry ladder for us kids: dresses, skirts, Sunday clothes, shorts, and the occasional lightweight jacket. A defining characteristic of the permanent press load was the need for hangers. Hanging up clothes can be a tricky business (something I apparently still have trouble with if the pile of clothes on the floor of my closet is any indication). However, there was one laundry rung none of us kids were ever permitted to reach: shirts. My father's dress shirts he wore for work were the only items of clothing my thrifty mother purchased at full price. These shirts were sacrosanct, and we kids were not to be trusted with their care. This load only my mother could handle.

I am not as particular as Mom when it comes to laundry. I don't pay attention to dryer settings. I don't lay my sweaters flat, or separate by color and fabric all that well (a fact that probably gives both my mother and mother-in-law the cold sweats). The truth is, I have a love/hate relationship with laundry. I love to visit my laundry line; I love to hang clean towels and sheets on the spinning laundry umbrella Nathan installed for me one Mother's Day. I love the sound as I snap the wet blue jeans straight and clip them to the line with wooden clothespins. I love the way towels and T-shirts make a whooshing sound as I gently spin the line around. I love the way all the socks look, clipped one by one to the line, alert and ready for inspection. I love the chance the laundry line brings me to stand outside in the fresh air and think thoughts without interruption, walking between the rows hidden from view as clean sheets billow around me.

Oh yes. I love the laundry line. But I hate the laundry itself. I hate how it piles up. How it is never-ending. How it multiplies faster than we can get it washed, dried, folded, and put away. And I hate how my children seem to think the dirty clothes bin in their room is a storage bin. Emptying their basket generally results in a slew of curse words. Things that do not get washed often or at all, like sports coats and pirate costumes, are piled on top of the clean clothes that have never been put away. Belts, the random shoe, and an occasional book. Even though their father and I have addressed this issue with them, with both our inside and outside voices, week after week. Which is why I want to pull my hair out and sit in sackcloth and ashes at the city gates when my boys tell me they have nothing to wear. I know it isn't true.

For our friends and family, it is no secret that the Greers like stuff. We are, as my friend Amy puts it, "stuff people." For years I tried to pretend it wasn't true, but lately I have come to embrace this truth with honesty and humility. We like our stuff. And it isn't because it is particularly nice stuff or expensive stuff. It's just our stuff. It's the stuff we like, stuff we have chosen, stuff we collect. We like books and movies, Legos and craft supplies, tools and vintage sheets. We like hunting gear, and reclaimed wood, and old china place settings, and stuffed animals. We like art, and vintage maps, and hats, and throw pillows (okay, so maybe I am the only one who likes those). We like stuff and we like collections. Maybe a little too much. Case in point: I recently had to tell my boys they could no longer "collect" every glass bottle that they drank a beverage from. When glass apple juice bottles began to accumulate next to the Mexican Coke bottles, I knew an intervention was needed. Now we have a rule for bottle collecting: only one of each kind of bottle is allowed in the house. Have mercy.

But dirty clothes and bottle collections were not the only things cluttering up my life. My anger and disappointment over losing the farm—my frustration that I was still here in this house—covered every surface of my heart. In one of my favorite books of all time, *An Altar in the World: A Geography of Faith,* Barbara Brown Taylor writes, "The great wisdom traditions of the world all recognize that the main impediment to living a life of meaning is being self-absorbed." Self-absorption, in the wake of The Awful Year was something I was all too familiar with. My deep and complete self-absorption was the emotional equivalent of my boys' laundry bin. We were not selling the house, we were not buying the farm, my life was going to stay exactly the same, and yet I kept revisiting these desires and disappointments over and over. Self-pity and entitlement were littered throughout my soul, and I was exhausted from the mess. I needed a serious spring-cleaning of the soul. I needed a tactile way to practice Being Here instead languishing in my desire to Be There.

In Jeremiah 29, after God has laid out the plan to the Israelites, after God has told them to stop their whining, to cool their jets, and to put down roots, there is this:

> "When you call on me, when you come and pray to me, I'll listen.
> "When you come looking for me, you'll find me.
> "Yes, when you get serious about finding me and want it more than anything else, I'll make sure you won't be disappointed." GOD's Decree. (Jer. 29:12–13 MSG)

"When you get serious about finding me and want it more than anything else." Those words were convicting arrows to my heart. It didn't take much scraping at the surface to realize that finding God was not what I wanted more than anything else. Finding a new life? Yes. Finding God? Well. . . .

But there it was. *When you get serious. . . .*

Hmmm.

Simplicity and fasting seem to be implicit in any talk of monasticism. They are rooting practices—practices that help one stay connected to the present moment, practices that call us out of the daydreams of Could've Been or Should've Been or Maybe Will Be. Practicing simplicity and fasting are considered historically to be serious ways of seeking God. Both practices are Lenten in nature. They are the sorts of disciplines that work to prepare our hearts and our lives for the work of the Holy Spirit by making space, clearing out the clutter and cobwebs and junk drawers of the soul. When we seek to simplify our lives, either by getting rid of our stuff or paring down our commitments, we are seeking to create space. Similarly, when we fast, be it from food or drink, entertainment, or some other seemingly superfluous habit, we are making space. And when we do these things with intention, when we purposefully remove an element from our life, we create within ourselves a wide opening through which God can come and move. Backwards as it seems, sometimes the best way for us to move away from ourselves is to look deeper within. Fasting requires us to do the paradoxical work of paying attention to the smallest details of our lives in order that we may forget ourselves. In other words, it helps us to get serious.

A few years ago my very brave and adventurous friend Alison and her family of six moved from North Little Rock, Arkansas, USA, to Aberdeen, Scotland. They moved so her husband could work on his doctorate in divinity, and so their children could learn a little bit more about what life was like outside of a southern, Christian, middle-class, American bubble. Before leaving, Alison and Taido sold most everything they owned, storing just a few precious boxes in Alison's parents' attic, cramming the rest of their material possessions into their suitcases and backpacks. I am pretty sure Alison, known for her baking prowess, crossed the great pond into her new life without even a rolling pin in her possession. Talk about simplifying.

Scotland, even though it is most definitely a first-world country, is still very different from America. With four kids ages eight to seventeen, a tight budget, and a three-year visa, my friends' housing options were limited. Eventually they found an attached house with just-barely-but-yet-adequate places for them to all lay their heads. The house also came with two toilets and a fitted kitchen (not always the case in Europe, as I learned binge-watching *House Hunters International* on HGTV). Alison's kitchen did include a stove (though not much bigger than an American hot plate), a sink (okay, so she says it's the size of a mixing bowl), and a clothes washing machine—hurrah! But no clothes dryer. Alison would have to dry her clothes—and the clothes of the other five people in her house—on her laundry line. Every time. Every load of laundry.

Apparently the lack of clothes dryers in homes is common in Scotland, something I find perplexing, since the Scottish climate is so wet. In Aberdeen, where Alison and her family live, there is some sort of precipitation fifteen days a month on average. Every month. This makes drying laundry outdoors a bit of a challenge, and often Alison's house is covered up by jeans and T-shirts and sweaters and underwear spread out to dry wherever she can hang or lay them.

Alison's family is familiar with adventure and rough living conditions—they did live out of a pop-up camper in the Pacific Northwest for one summer, and they are avid hikers and campers, so wet clothes are not altogether unfamiliar as part of an adventure. However, damp clothes as part of an everyday never-ending normal? That is another thing altogether. In fact I couldn't even imagine not being able to dry the laundry in a dryer indefinitely. Not even for my family of four.

Back in Arkansas, in a great act of empathy and solidarity, Alison's mother, Julie, had decided to forgo her own dryer, for one whole year, something I found incredibly endearing. Inspired by Julie, and desperately missing Alison, I decided this would be my stripping away, my fast. This would be my experiment in slowing down, digging in, and practicing simplicity. For one month I was going forsake my modern dryer in the climate controlled atmosphere of my home with a willing and open heart. I would offer up this interruption as an "assigned measure to God of my own will *with the joy of the Holy Spirit*," as St. Benedict wrote, hoping to create a deeper "spiritual longing" to live more like Christ, creating an open space for the Holy Spirit to work within me as I stripped away the convenience of shoving laundry from one machine to another.

When I committed to this monthlong process, I didn't really consider how much dirty laundry we could accumulate in a month's time and, in retrospect, perhaps I (and by I, I mean my whole family) should have fasted Jen Hatmaker-style from wearing so many clothes. If I was any sort of smart, I would have given everyone seven items each to wear during the fasting month. And I would have gotten all the laundry clean before the month even began. But I am not that kind of smart. I am the kind who starts a month without a dryer with twenty loads of dirty clothes sitting at her feet. I'm the kind who decides to fast from her dryer without considering little logistical details such as the speed it will take clothes to dry in April in Arkansas on a laundry line versus how long a washing cycle takes. Or even what the weather will be like in April (anyone know the old rhyme "April showers bring May flowers"?). Those sorts of practical thoughts just didn't appear on my radar. No, in typical Jerusalem fashion, I was enraptured with my spiritual fantasy, thinking such lovely thoughts as, "I will go out to the laundry line, I will commune with God, I will pray for Alison, it will be lovely and rooted in simplicity! I will be just like a monk! Or Cinderella with the birds! I will love my life again!"

This is how I began, Cinderella and monastic delusions abounding, making my way slowly toward the washer by sorting all the clothes into piles just as my mother would have, beginning my first load with a song in my heart. Once the first load was washed I gathered it all up in my super cute laundry basket and headed out the back door, trying not to step in dog poop or trip over broken toys scattered all over the back patio as I made my way into the garden and over to the line, and began to hang up my laundry, enjoying the cool afternoon air, and praying for Alison. I prayed she would be graced with patience in the midst of her situation, and that the sun would shine brightly over Aberdeen, thoroughly drying all her clothes that day. Clipping my boys' T-shirts to the line, I prayed she wouldn't be lonely, that she would make friends, that her kids would have a good day at school. And then, feeling rather proud of my spiritual and physical sacrifice, I went inside to my 1,800-square-foot house with central heating and air, started the second load of laundry, had some dinner, watched some television, and checked in on Instagram.

An hour later, the sun almost done setting, I went back outside to hang the second batch of laundry only to discover that the first load wasn't anywhere close to being dry. It was then I noticed a twinge of humidity in the air, but I dismissed it as typical Arkansas weather and went about hanging the second load next to the first, deciding to leave both loads on the line overnight just to make sure they got good and dry. "I'll take it down in the morning before I go into work," I thought to myself.

Somewhere around three in the morning, when the thunderclap woke me from a dead sleep, I realized with a sinking feeling that my laundry was not going to be dry by morning. And as it turned out, those two loads wouldn't be dry for several days. But they did go through several "rinse" cycles courtesy of Mother Nature. It was only after the third or fourth load of laundry I hung out to dry was doused in a rainstorm that I began to doubt the wisdom of trying this fast during the month of April. The only consolation was that my experience of trying to get my clothes dry in such wet conditions was probably closer to what Alison was actually going through in Aberdeen than if I had gone dryer-free in June. Only she had six people to clothe and I had four. How did she get everything dried? In a text conversation, this is what she said when I asked:

> Ugh. I have a crazy tedious system for getting clothes dry. Mainly I can only dry about 6 things per day in the winter and so everyone MUST wear their clothes for several days. Which we all do. I almost never wash my own clothes except for underwear bc I know what a pain it will be to get them clean + dry. :)

If we are diligent, with the help of a dryer, we can get six *loads* done in a day, and here Alison was talking about six *items*. During my dryer-free fast, I was lucky to get one load completely washed, dried, folded, and back in our drawers within a week's time. This way of drying the clothes on the laundry line might be "simpler" but it sure was less efficient and much more frustrating.

Still, I forged ahead, committed to loving my friend from afar, trying my best to put myself in her shoes, honoring her struggles, and trying to embrace the lessons of the fast and simplicity. Trying to find meaning in the going slow, in the thwarted plans. Of course not everyone in my house was a fan of this project. Toward the end of the month, during a particularly long rainy stretch, my husband finally looked at the mountain in the laundry room and asked imploringly, "So how long are you going to do this?" Succumbing to the pressure, I washed and dried a solitary load of underwear and towels, but I felt guilty the whole time, even though I firmly believed that if Alison were in my shoes, she would have done the same thing.

Soon enough the fast ended, and I went back to the dryer and gave a great big prayer of thanks for this blessed convenience as I started shoving our clothes in and out, in and out of our huge machines once again. I yelled again at the boys about their sports coats and their pirate costumes, and shook my fist toward heaven as I pulled out still-folded jeans from the bottom of the basket. Then and there, standing on Mount Dirty Clothes, I made the commitment to myself that somehow, come hell or high water, as a family, we were going to learn gratitude for all the things we had, and that we would show our gratitude by doing a better job of caring for the things we had been given. And if the volume of stuff—including clothing—was larger than we could manage with care, then we were going to do some purging of the excess until we had a "refreshed sense of what we have," as Robert Farrar Capon so wisely wrote.

Through fasting we have the opportunity to become acutely aware of all the ways the very thing we are trying to let go of consumes us daily. By letting go of the dryer, by stripping away this one bit of convenience, I was suddenly aware of just how much excess we had in our home. Not only did we have too many clothes, we also had too many of everything else. Too many toys, too many books, too many craft supplies, too many boxes of junk stuffed into the attic.

This year for Lent I gave up shopping—no clothing, home goods, books, craft supplies, or shoes. No trips to my favorite thrift stores, no one-click Amazon shopping. It wasn't until the option to buy was removed that I realized just how much space shopping—and thinking about shopping, and planning for shopping, and accidently shopping (hello, bargain bins at Target!)—took up in my life. From Instagram shops popping up in my feed, to the daily barrage of sale notices in my e-mail, to my weekly perusal of the local thrift shops, my compulsive checking of Craigslist, and the innocent click-throughs on a decor blog post, my days are apparently inundated with opportunities to shop nonstop. And even the process of choosing takes up space. Do I even bother opening the Decor Steals e-mail? Should I swing through Home Goods after I buy crickets at PetSmart? Should I order that new book now, or wait until I have finished the stack next to my bed? Even deciding NOT to shop was taking up space in my day because every e-mail, every store, every link, demanded a decision.

Fasting from the dryer created this same sort of awareness. Without an easy solution to keep our clothes clean, I became aware of just how many clothes we had. When you hang your wash on a laundry line item by item, you can count every T-shirt, every pair of jeans, every sock. With the tenth white T-shirt, or the umpteenth pair of shorts, you begin to wonder if just maybe you have enough. And if even, maybe, you have too much. A lightbulb comes on and you realize: *Huh, maybe the kids' clothes never get put away because they have more clothes than they can cram into their chest of drawers.*

Doing laundry in this protracted, long-suffering, drawn-out way, I became aware of how much excess we had and how dependent I was on being able to do things quickly and easily. It became glaringly obvious how the quick and convenient things in my life allowed me to live on the perilous edge between a balanced existence and one of harried exhaustion. The very machine that was created to relieve women like me from the shackles and burden of housework had become a crutch that allowed me to cram my days even fuller. In typical human fashion, I had taken this gift of time-saving technology and impaled myself upon it.

No wonder I was so devastated when my easy and convenient plan to run away from my life backfired. Easy and convenient is always my fallback plan. Easy and convenient is the very thing I count on to pull me out of the messes I continue to make in my pursuit of Doing All the Things. But all too often easy and convenient insulates me from needing to create space for the Holy Spirit to work on my heart, from facing the clutter of self-absorption covering my heart.

Living slower, fasting from convenience, taking better care of our possessions, doing the work needed to declutter our closets and our hearts, showing up at the laundry line again and again, day after day, to face the truth about our lives, to pray and to ponder. . . . These habits might not be the most efficient way to do life, but I think maybe they are the better way. Slow as they may be, they may bring about the most growth, bring us closer to wholeness, and strengthen our character. The Desert Father Abba Moses is often quoted as having said, "Your cell will teach you everything," and standing here looking at the pile of dirty clothes, I wonder if the same is true for our laundry rooms.

Jemimah's Homemade Laundry Soap

Using a laundry line might not be an option for you, or maybe fasting from wearing too many clothes isn't really something that interests you either, but making your own laundry detergent, even just one batch, can be a great lesson in both simplicity and slowness. Every time we choose to do something that is hard because we know the good it will produce in us, we are fasting, fasting from convenience. This can be good for both our kids and us, and this project is a good one to get kids of all ages involved in, and a great opportunity to start the conversation around the stewardship and care of our material possessions.

NOTE: Please be sure to read and follow all handling and care instructions for each ingredient listed below.

Ingredients

2–3 bars Fels Naptha soap
(I like 3)
1 large box Borax (4 lbs. 12 oz.)
1 large box Arm & Hammer
Baking Soda (4 lbs., roughly
5 cups)
1 large box Arm & Hammer
Super Washing Soda (55 oz.)
1 large bucket OxyClean (5 lbs.)

Directions

This will make 4–5 blender batches.
- Cut Fels Naptha soap into half a dozen cube-ish sections.
- Section out the bar soap in even batches.
- Get your blender ready.
- Add a few cubes of bar soap to the blender, then add a little bit of each powder into the blender.
- Keep layering the soap and powders like a trifle until the blender is 3/4 full.
- Blend! I pulse a couple times then set it to the high or chop ice setting.
- Pour the first batch into your airtight laundry soap storage container.
- Repeat until all powders and bar soap are blended and stored.
- Use one tablespoon per load.

Notes

Be sure to clean up your workspace thoroughly, as sometimes those powders like to float. Don't worry if each blender batch is not identical in proportions.

chapter 8

Stillness, Being, and Mending

You've no idea how quickly wilted wardrobes respond to kindness.
—*Make and Mend for Victory*, The Spool Cotton Company (1942)

When we are stricken and cannot bear our lives any longer, then a tree has something to say to us: Be still! Be still! Look at me! Life is not easy, life is not difficult. Those are childish thoughts. Let God speak within you, and your thoughts will grow silent.
—Hermann Hesse

The spring after I broke my foot I decided to give up multitasking for Lent. I was fresh off of the enlightenment of having discovered Jeremiah 29 and forging deeply through monastic writings. I was anxious to begin practicing as many spiritual disciplines as possible, eager to test my theory that there was a way to slow down without moving to a monastery. So I gave up multitasking. For the sake of the fast,

I defined multitasking as *doing more than one thing at a time by choice.* Under these terms I could no longer watch *Downton Abbey* while combing through Pinterest on my laptop, while simultaneously checking Instagram and Twitter on my phone. I was not allowed to read a magazine while talking to Nathan. I tried my hardest not to check the e-mail on my phone while walking from the parking deck to my office at the school. Or while riding in the elevator. No phone calls while driving. No folding laundry while watching a movie. Instead, I had to do each independently. One. At. A. Time.

This practice was brutal. And completely freeing. And to some degree it broke me. Something in me that had been running at warp speed for two decades suddenly cracked and split wide open, all that go-go-gumption spilling out. The mechanism inside my mind that told me to do more, run faster, and try harder had frozen up, and no amount of cajoling would get it running again. The Monday after Easter I tried to return to my multitasking, fifty-plates-spinning-in-the-air habits, but I just couldn't find the motivation to work at it any longer. I didn't like the feeling of being rushed, frazzled, and split into a hundred different shards of myself. Racing against the clock no longer held any sort of attraction. And even if I wanted to return to life at warp speed, my brain no longer worked that way. Suddenly, I realized I could no longer text my sisters, listen to Nathan explain his plan for a garden, and catch up on my blog reading all at the same time without losing my place in at least one of those conversations. Some days I couldn't even cook dinner and hold a conversation simultaneously. Whatever multitasking mojo I had before Lent was now gone. My brain had reformed itself into one whole piece, and it could no longer function at its old pace.

A longing for slowness and stillness had been ignited instead. I had tasted the smallest sample of a different way of being in the world, and I wanted more of the peace I had found during those six weeks.

God is mysterious, and in general I like this. I like that God is not manageable, not easily put into a box, that there are things about our Creator that make my brow furrow and my brain get fuzzy. Believing in something beyond my complete understanding seems appropriate. But liking the mystery and living in the mystery are not the same. Recently, while doing research for a writing project, I asked my seminary-educated father how he wrestles with the mystery of the Trinity. His answer? "We are encouraged to understand, but we are called to believe." Ah. Thanks, Dad. More mystery. The stillness I craved was also a mystery.

There is an idea in some church traditions that complete silence and stillness must be observed before Communion can be served, helping to change the pace of the energy in the room. At our church, after the bread and the wine have been blessed, after the Eucharistic prayer, the choir leaves its loft to come to the altar rail and take Communion first. This includes our organist. For a solid three minutes or so, with the exception of a cough or a baby's squeal, there is complete silence and stillness on the part of the congregation as the choir members and organist kneel at the altar rail and take the bread and the wine.

In the beginning, I found this practice to be very disconcerting. It seemed as if the whole service came to a grinding halt. No background music was being played, no singing was being done, no words were being spoken by priest or preachers. And then I began to notice the space this stillness provided for me to prepare for Communion—how the stillness and the quiet slowly worked into my mind and body, a deep awareness of every movement, every sound, the blessings given as each member took the wine and the host into themselves.

How often in our culture are there moments when a large group of people sit almost perfectly still, in silence, and wait for more than a moment? No phones out, no headphones in, no games being played, no screens being watched, no selfies being taken, no books being read, no feet tapping. I cannot think of a single one.

And yet, each week, I join others (as do people in houses of faith all over the world) and we sit and we wait. And then, after the choir and choirmaster and organist have had their meal and made it back to their loft, have opened their music and sung the first notes, only then does the stillness begin to break. And slowly and methodically, one row at a time, we all begin to make our way to the altar. And no one rushes (except perhaps for the preschoolers, who cannot contain their joy). No one shoves, or pushes, or complains about the long line. No one stares at a small screen in the palm of their hand as they move forward, one step at a time. In this stillness I often feel the Holy Spirit most. Here in this crack, in the pausing of the constant noise and work and doing that accompanies the rest of my life—this is where I find a deep and contented soul-rest.

I don't know what it is about me, but I can wear holes in my favorite cardigan sweaters faster than you can say, "Snap!" In fact I am fairly confident that from the moment I pay at the register, to the moment I hang the fresh-with-the-tags-still-on sweater in my closet, at least two barely perceptible holes will have begun their grand unraveling. These seem to multiply while I sleep. So you can imagine what happens when I actually wear them out in the world. Holes galore. But I hate to throw them out, these perfectly lovely, well-broken-in sweaters. They are security blankets disguised as clothing—comforting and predictable. Because of this I have begun to patch and stitch over the holes and rips.

In the months following my Lenten practice, my paternal grandparents both became sick and I knew chances were that we would lose one or both of them soon. I am their oldest grandchild, the first born of the firstborn, and I felt a duty, one borne out of love, to them and to the rest of my family to walk through this season at their sides, helping in any small way I could. And for many months, as both my grandparents went in and out of the hospital, then into the nursing home, it became abundantly clear that the best help I could give was to just show up. The best thing I could give was my presence. My stillness. My willingness to stop moving, stop trying to fix things, to change things, or to solve problems, and instead just be there. It was the only thing I had to give that was of any use to anyone. To be calm, to bear witness, to wait, those were the things they needed from me. I knew it would be a display of arrogance and selfishness to try to do anything other than just show up; trying to assert my task-related useful habits would just be serving my comfort and no one else's. So I showed up, and I sat my butt in the chair, and I waited.

Early on I found this could feel a little awkward and a little boring, a horrible thing to say about being present with your grieving grandmother or sick grandfather. But as someone slightly addicted to Getting Stuff Done, and whose identity rests heavily on Being Useful, this was a stretch. The feeling of being untethered to any task in the face of need was unbearable for me. Giving up multitasking for Lent had been a lovely practice, but even then I was able to do *something*. Sitting in hospitals and nursing homes, I was worried that if I didn't find something to do I would begin to twitch and shake like a drug addict in rehab on a made-for-TV movie.

But apart from getting my Nana some water, or waiting for my turn to hold my granddaddy's hand, there were very few things I could do. I didn't want to spend the whole time on my phone, scrolling through Facebook or Twitter, though I did occasionally check in to make sure the Internets were still arguing with themselves. My hands needed something to do so my mind could settle itself down.

So I began hauling around my ginormous stitching bag with me everywhere I went. Whether I was sitting in the hospital room, the nursing home, or my grandparents' house, I would pull out my old battered cardigan, cut pieces of scrap fabrics to patch holes, replace buttons, mend tears. The repetitive motion of running the stitches in and out of the fabric, the gentle smoothing of wrinkles from the patches, the feel of the worn knit sweater, almost paper thin in places, gliding across my hands as I shifted to the next rip in need of repair: these motions were familiar and comforting. With each stitch I could feel the tangled knots of questions and restlessness begin to unfurl, and a gentle soothing, even reassuring quiet begin to hum ever so softly, right below my sternum. My heart was opening little by little past the fear of being useless, and in the place of fear something new was taking form. Something Nobel Peace Prize winner Dag Hammarskjöld described as "a center of stillness surrounded by silence." I felt a certain quietude fall on my mind and my heart, like one of those weighted therapy blankets, settling down everything nervous and jumpy inside me.

In the end it was my granddaddy who died that year. My siblings, uncles, cousins, parents, friends, and I had sat by his bed for a week, saying one goodbye at a time. Across town, my Nana lay in bed, in a nursing home, recovering from a broken hip, unable to travel the last leg of his earthly journey with him. During the weeks immediately preceding and following Granddaddy's death, I took to wearing down the road between our house, his hospital room, and the nursing home, bringing the holey-est of my sweaters and my stitching bag filled with fabric scraps, thread, and needles—the very trinity of sewing—with me wherever I went.

In the beginning, while he was still conscious and lucid, before hospice took over, there was conversation and sharing stories, sweet laughter and spoonfuls of ice cream. But as the days wore on, the room filled with the weight of the inevitable, and Granddaddy began his exit into another mystery, one I try to understand but can never fully grasp.

During the final late night shifts, we took turns holding his hands, checking our e-mails, discussing his vitals, and waiting. I would pull my cardigan out of my bag and continue what I had started, needle and thread and tiny scraps mending tears big and small.

On other nights I drove across town to the nursing home, to fall asleep on a self-inflating bed, which automatically adjusted itself according to my weight to prevent bedsores. I was there to be present to my Nana, and stand as a witness as she watched the life she had known for sixty years disappear like a vapor without her consent. On those nights, I would pull out fragments of crocheted doilies to stitch and patch my sweater, as we watched Christian television's finest gospel singers and episodes of *The Waltons* on the big-screen television my uncles had brought. While John-Boy mulled life's quandaries, I sewed until my eyes grew too blurry to see the needle, until my stitches were so sideways that I would have to start over in the morning, or until the night nurses arrived to turn off the lights, tucking us in with their shuffling feet and brisk conversations.

It had only been in the months just before Granddaddy's illness that I had started to find a way to be in the presence of the sick and the dying. And it had only been by force of obligation that I made the effort to learn at all. Up until then I had avoided the hospital and the elderly like the plague. My discomfort around both was rooted in something I couldn't name. I had no conscious awareness of why; I just knew that when forced into a hospital, or cornered by an elderly neighbor or church member, a tidal wave of anxiety would rise up in me and I would flee from the situation in some blundering way. I feel the same sort of anxiety whenever I am talked into riding a theme park ride, and the ride tilts and turns and my stomach feels detached from my body. My primal flight instinct is so strong in those moments that if I wasn't strapped in I would probably jump from those rides, just as I ran from hospitals and the aged.

In hindsight, I can now say with all confidence that what I found stressful about hospitals and old people was my fundamental inability to fix any of it. I couldn't make anything better for anyone. (As usual, my problem in the situation is that I have made it all about me.) I always hunt for solutions, volunteer at conferences for fun. Sitting in a hospital room, completely helpless, with no agenda, is pure torture.

♡

As a good Southern preacher's daughter, I learned early in life that if I couldn't be the smartest/richest/prettiest person in the room, I could at the very least be the most useful. And as it turns out, I am good at that and I enjoy it. I like being useful; I love having a task. I liked being needed.

Stay on my toes, keep moving, keep fixing, keep managing. Useful people always have something to do and someone to talk to. But this way of navigating in the world can also be a crutch—a way to keep myself distracted and unfocused. Which is perhaps why I do it. A helpful, busy, useful person can do a lot of good in the world, and a helpful, busy, useful person can also drown in their own usefulness, suffocate from never stopping long enough to replenish their own spiritual and physical oxygen supplies. Usefulness and stillness can be partners, or they can be enemies, and until my granddaddy got sick, I only knew them as the latter.

Stillness isn't just a physical act; it is also an internal act. Stillness is about being present. About having the humility to say, "This isn't all about me or what I can do or what I can say." Stillness is about being intentional in how we divide our attention. It is about cultivating an awareness within ourselves.

Desert Father Antony said, "He who sits alone and is quiet has escaped from three wars: hearing, speaking, seeing. But there is one thing against which he must continually fight: that is, his own heart."

To an observer, my practice of stillness probably looks a whole lot like dawdling or inefficiency. Or, worst of all, daydreaming. My newfound love for sitting still and staring out a window, for multitasking as little as possible, for saying no to invitations more often than yes: I am sure it all seems counterintuitive. I know it is frustrating to those who would like to see me hustle more, but I just can't muster it up anymore. I think it has to do with age—I think it has to do with my season of life—I think it has to do with living long enough to realize how very little control I really have. When I was in my twenties and early thirties I was the type who might buy a T-shirt with "More Hustle" in shiny gold letters. These days I want the soft, oversized hoodie that says "Be Still" in gentle swishy lettering.

When I was a child, I spoke like a child, I thought like a child, I reasoned like a child; when I became an adult, I put an end to childish ways, writes Paul in 1 Corinthians 13:11 (NRSV).

Or as Maya Angelou put it, "I did then what I knew how to do. Now that I know better, I do better." I think of these two statements when I reflect on how I have transitioned from nonstop hustling to understanding the spiritual gift of stillness.

If I practice stillness out of a sense of entitlement or laziness, I am nothing but a glutton and taker. But if I practice stillness out of love, I connect to the life God has called me to live—one of future and hope—and I connect to the lives of those around us. But I must be intentional about folding the practice of stillness into the rhythm of my days in order to develop a sixth sense of when it is needed most. I think so often we think of love as doing. And a lot of times this is true. Love is filling the sippy cup and driving carpool and picking up milk and going to the wedding and throwing the party and serving at the shelter. Love can look like productivity, but love also can look like idleness—sitting on a nursing home bed, patching a sweater and watching bad Christian television with your grandmother while your grandfather slowly leaves the known world on the other side of town. Love can be waiting in silence while others approach the altar, allowing others to take all the time they need, receive all the blessing they need. Love can be a yes and love can be a no. Love can mean choosing to do one thing at a time in order to be present to each moment of our lives more fully. But most of all, love often can mean dying to our agendas, dying to our desire to look good and be popular, to our need to be in control and to win, forsaking efficiency and ease, and embracing the slow and often inconvenient realities of being present with others. St. Benedict addresses this issue by encouraging the brothers to support "one another's weakness of body or behavior" with great patience, showing pure love to each other, and forsaking what is best for oneself for what is best for one's brother. But in order to do this—in order to figure out what the needs of those around us are and how best to meet them, we have to stop chasing the Could Be's and Should Be's. Instead, like the Israelites in Jeremiah 29, we must learn how to settle into the life we have, be still, care for others, and rest in the waiting.

How to Patch-Mend
a Sweater (sort of)

Let me tell you from the start that I am not an expert mender. No one is ever going to give me an award based on my mending skills, so please do not hold me up to the light of the mending perfection of your great-grandmother. I will fail.

But I do all right, and I do what I set out to do, and this is to take something that has been loved a little bit thin in places and give it some new life. Spruce it up a little bit; make it acceptable for public outings once again.

As I mentioned earlier, my lightweight cardigan sweaters are the most prone to holes and tears, so these are the things I use to mend them:

- Embroidery thread
- Lightweight cotton fabric scraps
- Crochet doilies—all sizes. Sometimes I use them whole and sometimes I cut them up.
- Cast-off buttons
- Vintage hankies
- Embroidery needles
- Darning mushroom

Sometimes I place my patch on top of the hole or tear, but often I place it from behind. I like to create layers and patterns. Sometimes I will cut a scrap of fabric to look like a heart, or use a button and embroidery thread to create the look of a flower.

I almost never have a plan when I begin, I just start pulling bits and pieces out of the bag to see what fits, what works well with the sweater. Generally a theme will emerge—whether it is a texture theme, a color theme, or a pattern theme.

If possible, make sure all the fabrics you use are prewashed, and make sure not to sew any pockets closed (I may have done this a few times).

Occasionally I will use an embroidery hoop when adding patches to my sweater, but I have to be careful not to pull the sweater fabric too taut. If you do this you will get excessive puckering.

PART 3

DIGGING IN

chapter 9

Silence, Prayer, and Stitching

When life is heavy and hard to take,
go off by yourself. Enter the silence.
—Lamentations 3:28 (MSG)

Love is the voice under all silences, the hope which
has no opposite in fear; the strength so strong mere
force is feebleness: the truth more first than sun, more
last than star . . . .
—e. e. cummings

If I had to pick a quote to express how I think about myself, this might just be the one: "I myself am made entirely of flaws, stitched together with good intentions," by Augusten Burroughs. I am a broken, frayed-edged, mistake-making human, who mostly means well. Mercy, love, patience, hope are the fabrics that God has used to patch the gaping holes in my heart, the threads that have repaired the loose buttons and torn sleeves of my life, ripped and shredded by my choices, by the selfishness, by bitterness that seeps in slowly, corroding the warp and the weft of my soul.

Mended by the amazing grace of Christ as I am, there are still times when the frayed edges just completely unravel, when the mended, stitched-back-together places begin to wear thin again, when the stains and tears come too fast for quick repair and I am left raw and exposed—brittle to the touch, joy and hope long gone, cynicism and doubt left in their place, my faith and kindness disintegrating like an old quilt, forgotten and left to rot. When this happens, when I find myself in these seasons of unraveling, these threadbare moments, I have found that what begins to stitch me back together, what begins to mend my torn belief, is the gift of silence and the unformed prayers that rise up in the space created by both my own silence and the silence around me. There is a great and healing wholeness to be found in entering into the quiet.

We have never lived in the suburbs; instead, for most of our married life, we have lived in old neighborhoods near busy streets and bustling commerce, with bright lights and flashing sirens all around us. Until recently the constant noise never really bothered me. It was part of the background, the active signs of life happening, the price of living in town. But then, as you know, one spring I made the fateful decision to give up multitasking for Lent.

As part of my slow-down-and-dig-in practice, I decided it would be a good idea to see what life would be like if I did only one thing at a time. I wanted to know if by changing an external habit I could reset an internal rhythm. So I gave up multitasking — and all my senses decided to wake up, particularly sight and hearing. Suddenly I was much more aware of my external environment and its effect on me. All the sights and sounds I had previously been impervious to seemed harsh and invasive. The lights were too bright, the noise too constant. Working in a building that held almost a thousand children, lit by bright fluorescent lights, in a busy downtown area, was suddenly overwhelming. Not to mention that I was rarely alone.

This is how my day would go: up at 6 AM, get kids dressed, breakfast made (or poured, depending on how awake I was), lunches packed, myself dressed, and everyone—including Nathan—out the door by 7 AM. Drive together into downtown, park in a parking deck, then walk with the boys to their school and my work while Nathan walked another way to his work. And here we all would stay in the bustling downtown—the boys attending class, me working at their school, Nathan at his job a few blocks away—until 4 PM, when the boys and I would make it back to the parking deck, pick up Nathan from work, and fight our way home through traffic, back to our busy street, and our life together.

So you see, I was never alone, not really. And it certainly was never really quiet. No matter where I was—at home, in the car, at work, in the yard—everywhere I went there was noise, some of it loud, some of it soft, but all of it there. Under the strain of constant activity and a cacophony of sounds and vibrations, my body began to break down: headaches, stomachaches, fuzzy brain (as I call it), anxiety attacks, and deep tissue muscle pain; I was exhausted all the time, my immune system was shot, and I felt as sore as if I had lugged an elephant on my back every day. While there were many other contributing factors, I can say with all certainty that the constant influx of noise was a core issue. The physical pain I felt from external stimulation overload was very real and very present in my life.

This was the season when I began to viscerally crave silence and solitude, to fantasize about moving to the country as much for the quiet as for the cute farmhouse or the golden pond. I dreamed of a place of silence and peace—somewhere I could go to escape the constant buzzing and chatter that seemed to follow me everywhere.

I wanted to find the silence of a dark night with only stars. I wanted to hear wind in the trees, the sound of my breath exhaling. I wanted to know what rain on a pond might sound like. I wanted to stand and stare out across a field for no reason other than to be in the middle of the quiet, soaking in all the sun and breeze Mother Earth could spare. I daydreamed about having time to wander, time to walk aimlessly around my house in silence, lost in thin, wispy thoughts of no consequence. I needed protected space in my life—an agenda-free, demand-free, and most of all noise-free haven.

But time to daydream and walk about aimlessly around one's house and property isn't really on the American—or perhaps even Western Christianity's—agenda. Standing on a dock watching the rain hit the pond has no market value; sitting still, one's face turned toward the sun shining through a winter window, will not get the house cleaned; and lying stretched out on your front lawn gazing alone at the stars will not win any souls for Christ. None of these things produce anything, except an internal wholeness.

My mother has this great little plaque in her kitchen window that says, "Look Busy, Jesus Is Coming." I love that plaque because it sums up the way we have married the virtues of American industriousness and Christian service, creating the perfect storm of guilt-induced striving. Why do we see the discipline of silence and her sister disciplines—stillness, slowness, solitude, and Sabbath—as marks of weakness instead of marks of wisdom, especially in the Western world? Why does everything from our phones to our Pinterest boards seek to make us louder, brighter, busier, faster, and most of all, more productive?

I really understand John Cusack's Lloyd Dobler character from the great 1980s movie *Say Anything* when he says: "I don't want to sell anything, buy anything, or process anything as a career. I don't want to sell anything bought or processed, or buy anything sold or processed, or process anything sold, bought, or processed, or repair anything sold, bought, or processed. You know, as a career, I don't want to do that."

Like Lloyd, I was tired of the hustle. I was tired of all the buying and the selling and the processing. I wanted instead to be and to create and to live. But even those things were becoming harder and harder as my life grew louder and louder. And as my life grew louder, my body broke down; as my ability to parent and wife disintegrated, our home life began to break down, until I was doing only the bare minimum to keep people alive, clean, and fed.

♡

Parker Palmer writes that the "soul speaks its truth only under quiet, inviting, and trustworthy conditions." I had expected those conditions to come naturally when we moved to the country, but as we were staying put, I knew I would have to find another way to shut off the noise and enter into the quiet. I would need to learn how to create pockets and practices of silence where I was, within the confines of my life as it was, instead of how I wished it to be. Creating those trustworthy conditions would have to be as much an internal practice as an external one.

I began the process by making lists, enumerating all the noisemakers in my life I couldn't change: my job, the location of my house, the sharing of a home with other humans. Then I made a list of the things I could change: my own noisemaking, specifically my own talking, both self-talk and actual out loud talk; my commitments outside the home; and the media noise I invited into my day, including television, magazines, radio, podcasts, and, most significantly, social media.

Social media is its own special sort of noise. It is a 24/7 influx of voices and opinions. Between Facebook, blogs, Twitter, Pinterest, and Instagram, there was always someone talking, someone yelling, someone crying, someone laughing, someone succeeding, someone failing. The constant barrage of emotions and judgments had begun to overwhelm me—a sure sign of what I already knew: that my desperate desire for silence was reaching critical mass. I began by doing a mini-fast from each app, bringing it back to my phone when I felt as if I was healthy enough to read its posts without waves of anger, anxiety, or failure filling my chest.

But I knew my soul-ache need for quietude was deeper and more dire than could be answered by adjusting my social media intake. When anyone starts creating pockets of silence in their life, they begin by being silent. I knew I was going to have to be intentional about creating silent spaces in my life.

So, I pulled back on my speaking and traveling; I hunkered down at home more; I went out less. I slowed down my blogging and my social media activity, at times going completely radio silent as I tried to be for myself what I needed most from the world around me—quiet.

The practice of silence is an ancient one, found throughout Scripture and in the disciplines of the early church mothers and fathers who fled to the desert in order to hear God within. And yet, our busy modern lives and most of our busy modern faith practices are filled with noise. From the nonstop humming of our refrigerators, to the rock' n roll shows on many church stages, to the rapid-fire discourse on Twitter, our lives are filled with so much clattering. They say you know you have found the right person to spend the rest of your life with when you find the one you can sit in comfortable silence with—and yet we avoid sitting in silence with Christ, or with ourselves. How will we ever hear our own heartbeats, let alone the heartbeat of God within us, if all is noise? If all is rushing and panic and shouting? If all is running directly away from the very thing that should be the most natural? How can we find places of hushed peace within if we never visit?

In the Benedictine tradition, the practice of silence (generally observed during appointed times of the day) is meant to help monks learn to listen to God in the depths of their hearts, cultivating an awareness of the quiet moving of the Holy Spirit within them, and this will, in turn, help them be attentive to God's presence in others. This exercise of intentional silence, when practiced over time, creates an inward calm. The monks spend some of their monastic hours in solitude, but more often they practice silence in the midst of community, in their daily routines, as they go about work, meals, and housekeeping chores. Those who practice external silence again and again find that a path to inward silence begins to develop, a path leading away from the incessant clanging and banging of the mind, and toward the quiet and restorative presence of God within.

I was craving this kind of practice of silence—one lived out internally; accessible smack in the middle of my busy life. I needed to make room for the small, still voice of Christ within. I needed to develop a discipline of silence that could become a safe and familiar path, a path I could travel no matter the circumstance.

"When you call me and come and pray to me, I will listen to you. When you search for me, yes, search for me with all your heart, you will find me," says God through Jeremiah (Jer. 29:12–13 CEB). "There is no prayer without silence," wrote Mother Teresa. So prayer is where I decided to start.

Growing up an evangelical child of the 1980s, I struggled for years to have appropriate and intentional "quiet time." I tried fill-in-the-blank Bible studies and fervent prayers modeled after the evangelist I saw during revival season. I locked myself in closets, trekked out to lone tree stumps in the forest, and journaled in comfortable chairs by well-lit windows. I knelt, I stood, I lay prostrate. I tried when I woke up, I tried before I went to bed. But mostly during all of these quiet-time experiments, I fell asleep or felt bored, my mind wandering hither, thither, and yon. Of course, since I was a good Christian girl, my failure led to feelings of guilt (I must not love Jesus enough) and then resignation (I must not be wired to pray well). The funny thing is this: I was always praying, my days filled with a sort of constant conversation with God, as if God were a sort of imaginary—yet totally real—friend resting on my shoulder. It would be decades before I understood this as a legitimate way to pray—a way other people prayed as well—advocated most strongly by that quirky, dishwashing Carmelite, Brother Lawrence.

But in my quest for silence, I knew I needed a more intentional way to pray. I craved the sort of richness and depth that comes from having a multitude of prayer practices. The time had come to embrace the practice of silent prayer.

Just as prayer goes two ways, so does silence. We must learn to both give and receive. We must choose to go quiet ourselves, and then to allow the quietude of the Holy Spirit to come and fill in the space we have made, filling our hearts with a rest and a peace we cannot access any other way.

Being a novice at silence, both practicing and receiving, I thought it would be helpful to have a tactile project, to help me resist the urge to fall asleep or wander in my thoughts. A project to pick up and work on when I begin to feel the anxiety of too much noise, too much commotion, and too much chatter and buzzing all around me. A project to keep my hands busy while I quiet my mind and move into my heart. Like the ADHD students I love and work with at school, I needed a fidget tool to keep my energy occupied, freeing my mind to take its time connecting to my heart, to my breath, to my inner listening ear.

Inspired by beautiful Tibetan prayer flags I had seen on the front porches of neighborhood houses, I decided I would create my own prayer flags. Traditionally, Tibetan prayer flags are hung or staked outside a Buddhist home to promote peace, compassion, strength, and wisdom, reminding those inside and outside the home to re-center their lives on these virtues. In desperate need myself of all those lessons (and more), I wanted to create flags we could hang in our home, flags that would serve as visual reminders of what we are to pray for, and as a visual blessing over our home and all those who entered.

I gathered scraps of fabric, loose buttons, embroidery thread, and lace. I chose words for our flags: Compassion, Stillness, Peace, Mercy, Kindness, Love, Hope. And as a magpie begins to build her nest, so I began my practice of praying through silence, one little scrap at a time. I practiced in doctor's offices and airport terminals, at family reunions, alone on my back porch, and sitting next to my kids while they watched *Dr. Who*. I practiced alone as much as possible, and when not possible, I practiced in the middle of chaos. I practiced on road trips, on vacations, and late at night in bed. During these times of stitching I rarely spoke; instead, I practiced being and receiving, sometimes saying, "Come, Lord Jesus, come," as I threaded my needle and applied the first stitch.

"Remember the great value of silence. Each day there must be time for silence, even in our prayers and meditation. There must be time within when we neither speak nor listen, but simply are," writes John McQuiston II in his beautiful book on the Benedictine way of living, *Always We Begin Again*.

Over time I have found that the simple act of sitting and stitching, intertwining the needle, fabric, and thread, up and through, down and up again, provides a wonderful rhythm for letting go of words and opinions, for releasing the compulsion to respond to everything I see and hear and feel. Instead I am simply here, open, waiting, quiet. There is a wonderful beauty in not having to react to every sound I hear, in not being particularly productive, in stopping at intervals, looking up from my handiwork and staring out through a window, noticing the play of my boys, the smells coming from the kitchen as Nathan sautés onions and garlic in butter, the way the afternoon light dances on the countertops.

Needle and thread in my hand, I can be simultaneously present to and removed from the activity around me. In these moments of sitting and stitching, occasionally listening and looking, often having to undo several minutes' work to correct a problem, I can let go of the pressure to fill up the air around and within myself with words and thoughts.

Also, I noticed the change in my physical presence in those moments. During these times of stitching and silent prayer—of open receiving—a calmness runs through my blood and my heart. My breathing becomes slower, deeper; muscles relax, tension releases.

There in this silence, in my stitching and waiting, in my mending and quiet, I finally heard the heartbeat of God within my own chest. In those moments, I discovered I could simply be—as I was, where I was—and the world would not collapse around me. Slowly and steadily, one stitch at a time, I beat a path from the frenetic noise overload of striving and failing, to an inner quietude of love and grace. And it was sitting in this place of love and grace that I found the courage to accept what I had tried to ignore for so long: I was not ready to go, because I was still learning how to stay.

Running away to a farm may have brought external quiet into my life, but the loud shouting to Be More, Do More, Go Faster would have remained deep within me. The truth is, had we moved, I likely would have polluted the new space with my frenetic pace, with my desire to turn our move into great blog fodder in an attempt to win the online attention contest.

I would have missed out on the great gift of learning how to move and breathe and have my being in Christ, quietly, slowly, one stitch at a time.

Prayer Flag Craft DIY

Since I began working on my flags (an ongoing project), I have found this to be a great way to teach both silence and active prayer to my kids. Despite (or perhaps because of) this age of technology and fast motion, kids are drawn to this slow craft—the idea that they can make words and pictures out of piles of string and scraps seems to touch a chord in them. Teaching them stitching as a way to practice silent prayer also helps to reinforce the idea that prayer doesn't have to look a certain way or fit a certain mold—these prayers are just as valid as the ones we pray as a family at the dinner table, or as a community in church each week. Any person who can hold a needle or write with a pencil can make these flags. And if your kids are too young to do either, let them help by choosing the fabrics and colors. Encourage teens to make their own set for their bedroom, or as gifts for friends.

Supplies Needed:

Fabric scraps (for the basic flag shape you will need)
Embroidery thread
Embroidery needles (not too thick)
Spare buttons, small fabric scraps, and other bits and pieces (I used small doilies on some of mine)
Embroidery hoop
Pencil

1. To get started, put your flag fabric in an embroidery hoop.
2. Pick one word or phrase you would like to have on your flag. (Maybe use the Fruits of the Spirit or a favorite song lyric for inspiration.)
3. Write this word or phrase in pencil on your fabric.
4. Then "trace" the word with your embroidery thread using a chain stitch.[1]
5. Next, add all your other embellishments—buttons, fabric shapes, old jewelry, etc.
6. While you are sewing, say a prayer inspired by your choice of words. Pray those words over your home, over your family, or over someone you know who has a

---

1. http://sublimestitching.com/pages/how-to-chain-stitch

need in that area. You can also sing a song or recite a bit of poetry as a prayer while you stitch.

7. Once you have completed all your flags, simply fold the tops of each flag over, stitching a two-inch rod-pocket for the twine or ribbon to be threaded through.
8. Finish by hanging them somewhere prominent in your house!

And remember—this isn't about being perfect. There is no shame in wonky letters and rough edges and loose buttons. Prayer flags—like prayers—are to be real and authentic.

chapter 10

Sabbath

Listen! The Lord, the Eternal, the Holy One of Israel
says,
In returning and rest, you will be saved.
In quietness and trust you will find strength.
 But you refused.
—Isaiah 30:15 (VOICE)

There often comes a time in the life of the members
of "society" when they grow a little weary of the
ceaseless round of teas, balls and dinners, and for
such I would not hesitate to recommend a "picnic."
—Donald Ogden Stewart, excerpt from the 1922 etiquette
book *Perfect Behavior: A Guide for Ladies and Gentlemen in
All Social Crises*

Keeping the Sabbath is one of those spiritual disciplines that for years seemed antiquated, elusive, and somewhat misogynistic to me. My first impressions were formed by a little story in a children's biography of the missionary Lottie Moon, a Southern Baptist missionary to China in the early 1900s. As a girl growing up in the Southern Baptist world, I found each and every story of a strong woman leader within our tradition compelling, and I loved Lottie best. She was my kindred spirit, a woman doing work for Christ in her own way, fighting for women to have a voice in leadership, giving away all her food and money to the point of dying herself from starvation. The story I remember most vividly is of Lottie breaking her family's strict no-work-on-Sunday Sabbath rule. This rule prohibited any cooking, the result being only cold sandwiches or leftovers from the larder could be served. Lottie, thinking the rule was old-fashioned and silly, feigned illness and stayed behind from church one Sunday in order to prepare a large, hot, delicious meal for her family. Of course Lottie's choice landed her in a lot of trouble, but I thought it was magnificent. Reading about her rebellion, my budding little feminist self cheered her on, excited to see her break the Sabbath, which seemed to me just another meaningless rule by men to bind and hinder women from making their own choices. After all, what did God care if one cooked on Sunday or not? Wouldn't God be more in favor of you serving your family joyfully rather than being miserly and falsely pious? Jesus healed the sick on the Sabbath. Why were religious people always trying to make extra rules?

For a while, this is how I thought of the tradition of keeping a Sabbath: falsely pious, rigid, rooted in legalism, and not of any interest to Christ.

That is, until I had kids. Years and years later, a mother myself, getting up to make another round of breakfast and lunch and bottles and pots of coffee, it occurred to me that perhaps it had been women who had made this rule, and perhaps Lottie's mother enjoyed having the day off from slaving over a hot stove! I began to see there was some wisdom in the idea of a Sabbath. Ironically, though, it would take me another decade to create intentional Sabbath practices in my home, as I was far too tired to try any sooner.

In those days of snotty noses, sippy cups, potty training, working full time, and never having enough money for All The Things, Nathan and I instituted a practice we called International Nap Time. There are only two rules for International Nap Time: (1) Everyone in the house MUST lie in their bed for the duration of the entire nap experience—no matter what; (2) children may not get up until they are told INT is over, UNLESS there is excessive blood, fire, or puking. No exceptions. No getting up to ask me questions about the universe, no asking me to fix your flashlight, no coming in "one last time" to tell me you love me. Just no. International Nap Time was sanity for me. I waited all week for Sunday to arrive, because I knew that after church and lunch came rest—a beautiful, long, deep, bone-healing, sometimes three-hour-long period of rest. Those naps saved my life more than once. But as our kids grew, International Nap Time fell away and became a memory—our pace of life increasing, moving so fast that we wore the bottoms smooth of our going-shoes. That's when I broke my foot.

So, when I began wrestling with the question of what spiritual disciplines we should put into practice, Sabbath rose to the top of my list. I knew that if we were really going to learn how to love our life and try to redeem it where we were, we were going to need to follow the pace of life God seems to proclaim all throughout Scripture. We would need some sort of Sabbath practice; but I needed a new way to think about it and approach it—a way beyond Lottie Moon and grumpy old men with their grumpy old rules.

This is what I imagined when I daydreamed about keeping the Sabbath: the day begins with sleeping late, warm and snug under a gloriously fluffy duvet and very clean sheets. When I finally wake up, I feel ten years younger and find myself joyously in an empty house. I spend most of the day lounging around eating rich cheeses, grapes, and really crusty French bread, followed by some dark chocolate truffles. I read my favorite books uninterrupted, and a bottle of red wine is always at my elbow. Off and on during the day I might take a nap, or two, go for a walk, or doodle with paints in my craft room. The day ends with a hot bubble bath and one more truffle, then I blissfully drift off to sleep with great ease, immediately in peaceful REM.

Apparently what I wanted was a spa retreat for me, not a Sabbath practice for my family. When I thought of what it would look like trying to keep a traditional twenty-four-hour Sabbath as a family, I imagined all the pushback I would hear. All. Day. Long.

Why can't I play on the Xbox? It's not "work."

Does this mean I can't listen to music on my phone either? You let me listen to music at bedtime and that's restful!

What about watching football? This doesn't apply to Sunday football, right?

What about Netflix? Can I watch Netflix? Lots of people watch movies to rest.

What about my homework? You know I have to use the laptop for my homework.

Why do I have to take out the trash? Isn't that work?

Does this mean I don't have to do my homework?

What time is this over?

I really did not want to go to battle with my family. I didn't see much benefit in trying to force something that was supposed to be restful.

I don't know when or why keeping the Sabbath went out of vogue with American Christians. Perhaps it had to do with the birth of tin lizzie and the allure of a Sunday afternoon drive, or the way radios began to quickly fill up American living rooms. Or how the invention of the television made watching a football game from the comfort of the sofa after a big Sunday lunch quite enticing. Or perhaps it had to do with the way the larger cities began to fill up with immigrants from all around the world, each group bringing their own traditions and customs with them, some of which did not include keeping a Sunday Sabbath. I imagine that, like most anything, the American Christian Sabbath faded away in increments as technology and population grew and morphed. What began as one leisurely drive, or one radio broadcast, or one store open downtown eventually became a day to get errands done, to catch up on the laundry, and to watch football while checking in on Twitter and Facebook, and stressing out over getting everything ready for the week ahead. And perhaps, if you are a Christian, going to church.

I have read a lot about modern Americans and their attempts at keeping the Sabbath. Some did all right—primarily those who didn't have kids under the age of sixteen living at home. But almost to a person, they had to make adjustments, modifications, allowances. Especially families with kids between the ages of five and fifteen. Double if they were any sort of minister or clergy or much-in-demand church volunteer—a struggle Nathan and I know well.

Growing up in a preacher's family meant we began preparing for Sunday morning on Saturday night: pink sponge curlers were applied to my head, a Sunday's best dress was carefully laid out, and my siblings and I were not allowed to have sleepovers or attend sleepovers because we had to go to bed early. Sunday is a day of worship, but in a minister's family, it is also a day of work—*the* work day; all roads leading to its arrival. For most ministers, Sunday is the most consuming, the most taxing, the most exhausting, and the most wonderful day of the week. The day when you "leave it all on the field," which is why most ministers I know leave the church parking lot on Sunday afternoons completely depleted of all interpersonal skills and energy.

Amid the flurry of curling irons, spilt cereal, diaper bags, and lost shoes, somehow my mother also began preparations for Sunday dinner: roast in the oven, salad made, potatoes boiled. Because my family only had one car then, we all had to go to church when my Dad went, except for the years when we lived next door to the church. Fits, fights, and tears were just part of the package as all six of us struggled to get out the door and on the road on time so my dad wouldn't be late.

After church was over—and by over I mean everyone had left the building and we locked the door behind us—we headed home and mom finished whipping up our wonderful hot Sunday dinner while Dad changed out of his Sunday best, and my siblings and I set the table. Once dinner was over and the tabled cleared, it was naptime for everyone. Dad dozed while the Cowboys played the Giants, the volume down low, and the rest of us headed to bed. Sunday naps were sacrosanct at my house and they were necessary, because as good Southern Baptists, we would soon be headed back to church for Sunday evening classes and services. Back home again around 7 PM, we would have breakfast-for-dinner and watch whatever Sunday evening show we could catch before bed. For our family, Sunday was not a day we played organized sports, went to birthday parties, or to the movies. Though I was never sure if this was because it was the Lord's Day or if it was because my parents were too worn out.

"It does seem to me that at least some of us have made an idol of exhaustion," writes Barbara Brown Taylor. "The only time we know we have done enough is when we are running on empty and when the ones we love most are the ones we see the least." When I broke my foot and landed myself on the couch for three months—stuck in a place I didn't want to be in, confronting a mess of a life of my own devising—I had to confess that I had made an idol of exhaustion, and I had to admit that the model of Christianity I followed had done the same. Somewhere along the way, Sold Out for Jesus had become Worn Out for Jesus. We had begun to equate busyness with our worth; we measured and judged our lives, our families, and our marriages by how many extracurricular activities we were all participating in. We measured our obedience to and love of God by how many small groups, ministry teams, mission trips, retreats, service projects, and church sports leagues we joined. Even the things we started as recreation became work. Our frenetic pace as we tried to Do It All made our play exhausting and our worship drudgery. We have made an idol out of exhaustion *in the name of Jesus, Amen*—a modern Christian martyrdom rising up to help us to justify our newest golden calf.

> "Don't let all those so-called preachers and know-it-alls who are all over the place there take you in with their lies. Don't pay any attention to the fantasies they keep coming up with to please you. They're a bunch of liars preaching lies—and claiming I sent them! I never sent them, believe me."
> GOD's Decree! (Jer. 29:8–9 MSG)

God's entire message to the Israelites in Jeremiah 29:4–14 seems to be: *Be Here Now. Be content and invested in the life you have, instead of wishing for a different life.* But much like me, the Israelites had a hard time receiving this message, and instead of digging in where they were, some of them even looked to "false prophets and diviners" seeking a different answer, perhaps looking for a magic formula to get what they wanted out of God.

For me, and maybe for you, the fantasies and lies I choose to believe—the messages I take in from so-called preachers and prophets of culture, social media highlight reels, church programmers (of which I am one), and marketing companies—are the ones that say busyness is next to godliness. And this idea, that we should strive to Do More, Be More, Have More, and Work More in order to have The Perfect Life, has fed into my core belief that I am not enough—that where I am is not enough, and that my life is not good enough.

If we are to believe both our culture and our religious institutions, the only way to succeed in life is to run ourselves and our families so hard, so relentlessly, so ragged, that we become shredded, depleted, shadows of who we are created to be: whole, loving, thriving people.

Like so many others around me, I had fallen for this lie of the get-happy-quicker gimmick-sellers, of the grass-is-greener soothsayers, and I had nearly driven myself and my family to the brink of insanity. I was no better than the Israelites in the book of Isaiah. I had refused to rest, refused to do my life at a sustainable pace, and most of all, refused to live the life God was offering me.

So what was the answer to this busy-is-better lie? How could I wean myself off my habit of running myself (and everyone around me) ragged, often in the name of Christ? What would it mean to rest in what is, instead of always chasing what could be?

In his book *The Supper of the Lamb*, Robert Farrar Capon writes this:

> The world exists, not for what it means but for what it is. The purpose of mushrooms is to be mushrooms, the purpose of wine is to be wine. Things are precious before they are contributory. To be sure, God remains the greatest good, but for all that, the world is still good in itself. Indeed, since He does not need it, its whole reason for being must lie in its own goodness; He has no use for it; only delight.

The purpose of a raspberry is to be a raspberry. The purpose of a cloud is to be a cloud. The purpose of snail is to be a snail. Things are precious first. God has no use for them, only delight in them. How amazing. Could this mean that naps can be just naps? And not a pitstop before the next event? If Capon got it right—and it resonates so deeply within me I cannot help thinking—then perhaps the purpose of rest, the Sabbath sort of rest, is to just rest. Just because it's rest.

Perhaps the reason we get Sabbath wrong—or have abandoned it altogether—is that we came to see resting as a highly inefficient way of acquiring fuel to do more, instead of a sacred call to restoration and wholeness. Maybe, before we can celebrate the Sabbath as God intended, we must first be willing to see rest as a precious gift instead of a useful tool.

♡

Nathan is also a preacher's kid whose Sundays looked almost identical to mine growing up. For most of our married life, we have both served at church on Sunday mornings—he in the band and I on staff or leading in some way. Because of this, our Sundays have looked both similar to and different from those of our childhoods: cooking large Sunday dinners was out, but naps stayed in. I wouldn't call this Sabbath keeping, not in the way I understand Sabbath to be. Those naps are not luxurious pockets of rest; they are desperate attempts to recoup all the sleep I have forfeited during the weekend trying to be as productive as possible. I take these naps in order to work more, work harder, get more done. This, my friends, is not resting; this is called fueling up. Rest and fuel are two very different things.

Which is why I decided to go back to the beginning and look at the first Sabbath. I went back to Genesis and read the story of creation again, falling in love especially with the phrasing in The Voice translation:

> Then God surveyed everything He had made, savoring its beauty and appreciating its goodness. Evening gave way to morning. That was day six. So now you see how the Creator swept into being the spangled heavens, the earth, and all their hosts in six days. On the seventh day—with the canvas of the cosmos completed—God paused from His labor and rested. Thus God blessed day seven and made it special—an open time for pause and restoration, a sacred zone of Sabbath-keeping, because God rested from all the work He had done in creation that day. (Gen. 1:31—2:3)

Savoring its beauty and appreciating its goodness. An open time for *pause* and *restoration.* Thus God *blessed* it. And God *rested.*

Blessed. Rest. Pause. Restoration. Savoring. Beauty. Appreciation. Goodness. These are the ways the purpose of Sabbath is shown to us. What if we celebrated Sabbath through these ideas? What if these were the touchstones for creating a Sabbath practice in our home?

♡

In his book *God in My Everything: How an Ancient Rhythm Helps Busy People Enjoy God,* pastor Ken Shigematsu writes, "The golden rule for the Sabbath is to cease from what is necessary and to embrace what gives life." I began to wonder: Instead of trying to reserve a whole day for a Sabbath, would it be possible—as a family and as individuals—to capture moments, minutes, and occasionally hours to embrace that which gives us life? How could I, alone and with my family, intentionally choose to pause and rest? To savor beauty? To appreciate goodness? To cease living and dying by our To-Do List and to instead embrace all that is good? How could we celebrate and enjoy what God has created? And not seek anything productive from the experience? Could we enjoy eating an apple for the sake of its being an apple, instead of for its fiber benefits? Could I sit on my couch and simply appreciate the goodness of its softness and presence? Could we have a picnic on our back porch and savor the juice of the rotisserie chicken as it runs down our chins? Could we sit there in silence side by side or in laughing conversation until the beauty of each family member is so obvious that we cannot do anything other than call the moment good? Could we put down our devices, lay down our heads, turn off our alarms, and rest until our bones are restored? Not in order to be strong enough to work again, but simply because rest is precious in and of itself? And if so, might this be a place we meet God, entering into the same rhythm and way of interacting with creation—through celebration, enjoyment, and delight?

I was willing to try. We began—slowly, occasionally, imperfectly, messily—to keep the Sabbath as a family. I am probably the least qualified Sherpa for this experiment, as Doing What Is Necessary has been my modus operandi for as long as I can remember. But Nathan and I did our best to be mindful as we looked for openings through which we could create Sabbath moments at home.

We stopped homework and chores to run and jump in our blow-up pool. Nathan set aside his very long honey-do list to help Wylie build a wooden sword. We took walks, we sat on the front stoop of our house and enjoyed the way the light filtered through the trees on a spring afternoon. We ate dinner around the table without our phones, laughing over who could tell the dumbest jokes. We sat on the porch swing and watched the chickens peck, peck, peck. Miles asked if he could make a smoothie and I said, "Yes! Sure! Mess up the kitchen! Enjoy the blender because it's a blender!" We had living room picnics and media-free evenings—which meant no media of any kind for anyone, adults included, between the dinner hour and lights out. We made cookies in the middle of the week, we skipped church and slept in, we took long Sunday drives to the country, and we took naps. Long, glorious, luxurious naps. Just because we could.

We began to embrace what gave us life instead of what made us productive. Keeping the Sabbath, albeit unconventionally, we created pockets of time to celebrate rest, creation, and each other throughout our week. And miraculously, these little pockets of celebration spilled over into our attitudes and habits, helping us to take down our idol of exhaustion, burning it in a fire of repentance, allowing a more whole way of living to rise from its ashes.

30-Minute Sabbath Practices

The Rules

Rule 1: Don't stress out.

Rule 2: There is no rule about how often you should practice Sabbath. Do it when you can. No beating yourself up about not doing it more often!

Rule 3: Sabbath practices really do work best when all devices are put away and turned off (adults too).

Rule 4: Everyone in the family should participate if possible—even grown-ups.

Rule 5: No murmurings of discontent.

Rule 6: End your Sabbath practice with a prayer of thanksgiving.

Sabbath practices will bring restoration when you are intentional about taking the time to pause and rest, when you choose to savor beauty, appreciate goodness, and celebrate your blessings. As a family, make a Sabbath Practices List. Begin by asking each other: "What brings our family life and joy?" Use those answers, then add more ideas from below if needed.

Picnic Kit

I f you think taking a picnic might be a fun way to celebrate Sabbath, right now, before you can change your mind, go ahead a prepare a picnic basket to keep waiting by the door for the first perfect spring afternoon or midweek evening when you need a little instant getaway. With a kit all ready to go, you won't have any excuse when the picnic mood strikes! Call a few friends, throw some blankets in the car, swing by your local grocer, and head to your favorite park for a simple picnic supper that will transport all of you to a much slower rhythm of life.

Don't feel much like leaving home? Have a picnic in your backyard or on the front stoop. The location isn't what's important; it's the simple act of doing something different, something out of your routine, that will help you take a break from all of life's demands!

Picnic Basket

1 large basket, vintage suitcase, or favorite backpack

Selection of mismatched cloth napkins (perhaps use the ones that have seen better days but are too lovely to toss?)

Jelly jar glasses

A tin can filled with inexpensive flatware (my favorites come from flea markets and dollar stores)

Melamine dishes for everyone, a few extra for serving

Salt and pepper shakers

A roll of paper towels

A decent kitchen knife

A comfy quilt or a large rectangular, flannel-backed tablecloth

1 can favorite bug deterrent

1 bottle favorite sunblock

Kite, sidewalk chalk, bottle of bubbles

Matches

Citronella jar candles

Hand sanitizer

Small cutting board

Straws

Easy European Inspired Picnic Meal

This is our favorite meal to grab at the grocery store if we decide on a picnic at the last minute. It is inspired by what I imagine a picnic in the rolling provincial hills of France would be like.

Loaf of crusty French bread

Bottled sparkling lemonade

Bottled water

Some fresh fruit—locally grown strawberries or peaches are favorites

Grape tomatoes

Package of fresh mozzarella

Package of classic hummus

Small rotisserie chicken

Spread the cheese, fruit and tomatoes out on your cutting board to serve. Use your bottled water to rinse your fruit and veggies if needed.

Leave the chicken and hummus in their containers, carving the chicken as needed. No need to stand on ceremony; this is a picnic! Instead of slicing the bread, let everyone tear off chunks.

Sabbath Prayer:

Blessed are You, Lord our God. Thank you for the gift of Sabbath and the restoration it brings. Thank for an open time to pause and savor the beauty of our lives. Help us to appreciate the goodness of this moment. Amen.

chapter 11

Manual Labor, Restoration, and Thriving

Question: What do you do before becoming enlightened?
Answer: Chop wood and carry water.
Question: What do you after you become enlightened?
Answer: Chop wood and carry water.
—Zen proverb

In a world where faith is often construed as a way of
thinking, bodily practices remind the willing that faith is a
way of life.
—Barbara Brown Taylor, *An Altar in the World*

Sitting there, waiting to sell the house, to buy the farm, to pull the escape cord,
I could feel our family life—our marriage, our parenting, our kids' relationships
with us and with each other—withering around me. Seeking a "better" life, we

had stopped tending to the life we already had. I had retreated to my bed and into myself, the kids had retreated into the vortex of Netflix, and Nathan was spending more and more time in the garage. In our disappointment and confusion, we had done the worst thing possible: we had abandoned each other.

In Jeremiah, God instructs the Israelites to stop waiting for things to change and to get on with the business of digging in and living where they are, and specifically, God tells the people to get married, have kids and grandkids. God tells the people to do this so they will thrive, instead of wasting their lives away waiting for someday to happen. *Get yourself into some covenant relationships, live in the now, do the work needed to flourish*, God says. *It is better to grow where you are than die wishing you were somewhere else!*

The day I registered Wylie for his last year of junior high my breath caught in my chest, and a cold panic began to take over my body—it hit me how little time we had left with our kids at home. We were down to years instead of decades, years I knew would fly by as the boys pulled further and further away. Sitting at my desk, staring at the Thank You For Registering Your Child notice on my computer, I realized we no longer had the luxury of waiting for someday to happen; someday was here. Now was the last chance Nathan and I would have to create the family life we had always dreamed of. City house or country farm, twenty acres or an urban lot: it no longer mattered. Time was rushing by like a mighty wind, shredding my heart into a thousand little ribbons. If we were going to thrive, then we had to get serious about obeying God's command and start living in the here and now as a family, as a team.

Like Phyllis and Sam Tickle, as I said in Chapter 1, Nathan and I had long wanted our boys to learn the lessons that come from working the land, digging into the earth, and putting shoulder to plow (or peddle to tractor.) We wanted to instill in our boys a respect for hard work they had missed growing up in the city. We wanted them to learn to how to sweat and wrestle and come out the other side proud of what they had accomplished. I especially wanted to impart the monastic philosophy of stewardship: that everything we have is on loan from God, and that, as we care for it, gratefulness and appreciation for all we have been given will grow. If the chief end of man is to glorify and enjoy God, then I wanted my boys to embrace and explore both aspects. I wanted them to learn what it means to glorify God by working hard to care for the things we have been given; and I wanted them to learn what it's like to enjoy the fruits of hard work, taking in the knowledge that God's love and care for them and all of creation far exceeds our love and care of our world and each other—even on our best days.

When I was still holding out hope for a move to the country, I had daydreamed of our family doing farm chores together. I imagined us driving tractors, harvesting crops, planting wildflower gardens, and pruning fruit trees, basking in both the glory and enjoyment of God's creation and our place in it. Apparently, I was under the impression that a change of Zip Code would result in a change of personality because, as we all know by now, I am not a yard-working, garden-planting, tree-pruning sort of person. But still, this all-hands-on-deck-family-chore fantasy was one I replayed often. But moving to the country was not happening, and our boys were continuing to grow. If we were going to teach our boys these lessons, we had to do so right where we were: on a small neighborhood lot, in the middle of the city.

This is how we found ourselves out back ready to tackle our overgrown yard on a typical Arkansas summer Saturday (read too hot, too humid, and too bright). Earlier in the morning, Nathan and I had rallied the troops. We ate a hearty breakfast, we dug out gloves, we brushed cobwebs off rakes and loppers, and we covered ourselves with a haze of bug spray. We were prepared to do some hard labor as a family. We were going to learn the value of sweat equity and enjoy God forever. Go team!

Within five minutes, Wylie had poked a hole in our classy blow-up pool, Miles had overheated, and I was literally lost in the weeds. Nathan had handed me some sort of yard tool and told me to get rid of "those vines," but I felt as if I had been dropped in the middle of a *Project Runway* challenge with only one needle. No, scratch that. I know I could figure out a *Project Runway* challenge. This was more like being dropped in the middle of a physics class with only a Tolstoy novel for help. I felt useless, foolish, ill-equipped, and out of my depth. We had barely begun and the boys and I were deflated and dejected. And Nathan (the one family member who excels at manual labor) was frustrated with us all.

After a few half-hearted attempts to cut down the vines, I threw in the rake, and retreated to the indoors and projects I understood: laundry, sweeping, cooking. Soon I heard the screen door slam and saw one boy dash through the kitchen on his way to the bathroom, not long after, the second boy walked through mumbling something about needing a new pair of socks. Each of us, with very legitimate excuses mind you, had managed to sneak our way back indoors to the easy life of air conditioning, leaving Nathan to tackle the vines and the punctured pool alone.

During lunch standing at the kitchen bar, Nathan said the thing neither of us had wanted to admit: "We don't need a farm. We aren't ready for a farm. Our house is a disaster and we can't even work on our little city lot together without it devolving into tears, meltdowns, and me working alone."

I hated that he said it—mostly because it was true. Our family was a big bag of mixed motives, bad communication, unclear expectations, and confusion. We were no better at working in our backyard than the people in the book of Genesis were at building the Tower of Babel. We wanted what was comfortable and familiar, and frankly, what was easy. We wanted the perfect Instagram life—the one where all the mess is cropped out and a filter makes everything look charming. But no life is that curated, not if it is alive and flourishing. Real life—the good life, a whole life, the kind of life we were so desperate for—is messy, and long, filled with hard work and sacrifice. And, most importantly, this kind of real life can only be lived out in community and mutual support. Just as the Velveteen Rabbit became "real" after a life of being worn down by the one who loved him most, so we become real when we live life together, facing both the joys and the hardships together, sharing in moments of laughter, tears, and sweat.

Jonathan Wilson-Hartgrove writes, "I am changed by the weeping and eating together, I am changed by the invitation to share another person's grief." To which I would add, I have also been changed by another person's healing.

Joshua, my younger brother by three years, had always been a mixture of emotions and extremes—especially as a child. Extremely happy, extremely frustrated, extremely sensitive, extremely kind—Joshua would take on the emotional weight of the world and whatever he felt, he felt it with his whole being. While I seem to have been born with the ability to gloss over pain and be suspicious of happiness, Joshua has always been able to live fully—allowing all the feelings in and all the feelings out. Giving it all away, holding nothing back, for better and for worse.

The winter he turned twenty, Joshua was living in my grandparents' basement while he flailed around trying to find himself, attending community college and partying entirely too much, feeling all the things. I have read that most addicts find their bad habits while looking for community, and my brother, perhaps the most relational being on the planet, was traveling full force down this road. Joshua would call me, lost in a haze of drugs, depression, loneliness, and confusion. My memories of those phone calls are sensory: I don't remember words as much as I remember impressions. When I think back, there is a dark room with only a pinhole of light at one end, and my brother's voice, lost and sad, echoing in the blackness that seemed to surround him at the other end. Those were scary phone calls for me, for both of us. And each time I hung up I wept, unspoken prayers—that he would hang on one more day—pouring through my tears.

But then the pinhole of light grew slightly brighter when my grandmother decided—by some miracle of mercy and grace, or because of her upcoming knee surgery—to send Joshua in her place on a mission trip to Honduras. She had signed up to go on the trip months before, but as the time to leave grew closer and closer she began to second-guess her decision; to not waste her deposit, she devised a plan to send my brother in her place. The plane tickets would be exchanged, his passport would be updated, and off he would go to a farm in Honduras, where he would work alongside local craftsmen to build a community building out of stones, mixing concrete by hand. So, one frosty January day, we loaded my pale, skin-and-bones brother, with his weary eyes and sideways smile, onto an airplane with half a dozen Presbyterians and sent him south for hard work and time away.

Two weeks later, the man who came off the plane was my brother as he was created to be. His skin, now a golden brown, radiated health. His eyes were clear, alert and lucid, his smile thick and hearty. He looked strong, confident, free. The physical work had been transformative. Something holy and mysterious had always happened to him when he worked hard, physically hard. Sweat and effort, and more sweat, and more effort, unlocked a peace inside my brother that sitting behind a desk never would. When his body was active, his mind—something that often moved faster and in more directions than he could process, and took detours down paths of internal destruction, fear, pain, and self-hatred—slowed down to a healthy speed. Bad Mind shut her filthy mouth, and Joshua's truest nature—the caring, funny, smart boy I had known—was able to grow and rise.

Joshua had needed to go to Honduras because he needed to work with his hands; he needed to sweat out every last narcotic and breathe in every bit of fresh air. He also needed to work in community and be loved. I wouldn't know until much later how much the leader of the trip, a man named David Gill, had cared for Joshua. Had led him, looked after him, helped him navigate a foreign land, then pushed him to grow. This relationship was integral to my brother's healing. There was a beautiful dance between David's gentle prodding and the manual, body-breaking labor, which began to break the patterns of lack of purpose, Bad Mind, and self-destruction in Joshua. One without the other, only manual labor or only friendship, and the process would have been incomplete; together, they were the healing balm so needed for my brother's wounded soul and weary mind. Together they gave Joshua motive and purpose, comfort and challenge, the opportunity to rise to the work and to David's expectations. "Healing is impossible in loneliness; it is the opposite of loneliness," wrote Wendell Berry in *The Art of the Commonplace: The Agrarian Essays.* In Honduras, part of my brother's aloneness was erased by David's friendship and part by the camaraderie my brother found with the local workers. The masonry workers Joshua worked alongside were so proud of their skill, so grateful for the opportunity to work, that they sweated and toiled day after day with a spirit of joy about them, infecting my brother with their gladness and changing his work ethic forever.

To my dying day I will believe that this trip saved my brother's life. It allowed Joshua to both detox and refill. Losing shadows of despair and finding sources of hope within himself, he came back a transformed man.

Seeing this transformation in my brother was the beginning of my understanding what St. Benedict meant when he said, "Idleness is the enemy of the soul."

When we use the toil of our hands and not only our minds to bring newness and restoration to the world, we become part of God's healing process in creation. When we dig in the soil and plant a seed, we enter into a cycle of restoration that produces wholeness in us. Our bodies are restored by the tilling and the harvesting, our minds are restored by the space that such repetitive works opens up within us, the earth is restored by the nutrients provided through the plant, and our spirits are revived as we become better stewards of what we have been given. And when we enter into this work with grateful hearts, when we see our work as a way to give thanks and praise to God, we are transformed further, growing more in Christlikeness with every push of the shovel, every pluck of a weed. After all, as Jana Riess writes in *Flunking Sainthood*, "Redemption is physical. God doesn't stand around watching the world go to hell in a handbasket; he gets his own hands dirty by sending his son to heave us from the muck."

I believe there are lessons only manual labor—the use of large muscles, intentional movement, and sweat—can teach us. Mary Ellen Chase once wrote, "Manual labor to my father was not only good and decent for its own sake but, as he was given to saying, it straightened out one's thoughts." This is how it has always been for Nathan. Something happens when he is outside, swinging a hammer, tilling a garden, or chopping wood. Somewhere in the midst of the repetitive movements, the focus on the task at hand, and the fresh air, he begins to breathe deeper, think clearer, and feel more centered.

St. Benedict encouraged practices of prayer even during the working hours, believing that all things should be done to the glory of God—with God, for God, through God.

Which is why, when our family attempted to do manual labor together, our plans were doomed before we ever began. Except for Nathan, no one was willing to sacrifice their comfort. The boys and I had not even a smidgen of a grateful heart about the idea. Nowhere in my spirit was I doing the work as unto God. I was not hacking vines with a spirit of gladness; I did not approach our chores as a sacred endeavor.

That day in the backyard, Nathan and I also had failed as leaders, as parents, as a team. We were not doing the work with one accord. We had gone in our own directions, leaving the other to flail about on their own, and our frustration with each other was palpable. "Complaining is the acid that shrivels our souls and the soul of the community around us as well," wrote Joan Chittister in her exposition *The Rule of Benedict: A Spirituality for the 21st Century.* That day our souls and our family community were shriveled to the size of raisins. Unlike David working alongside my brother, Nathan and I had done a lousy job with each other and with our boys. We had not been supportive or encouraging; we had not stopped to help one another; we had not practiced what Benedict calls "Mutual Obedience." We had not sought to serve one another without grumbling; we had not sought to lighten each other's burdens. So when Nathan said we were not ready for a farm, I knew he was right, but I wasn't ready to admit it out loud. I wasn't ready to admit defeat or failure.

But it was the truth, and the seed of it nestled deep down inside me for months as I wrestled with the knowledge that before we could move forward we would have to do a better job of thriving right where we were.

chapter 12

Mutual Support, Starting Seeds, and Gardening

A family is a place where minds come in contact with one another. If these minds love one another the home will be as beautiful as a flower garden. But if these minds get out of harmony with one another it is like a storm that plays havoc with the garden.
—Gautama Buddha

Gardens are not made by singing 'Oh, how beautiful,' and sitting in the shade.
—Rudyard Kipling

There is a story my mother tells about me at least once a year and it goes like this: when I was a little girl I was easily persuaded by commercials. Make it look good on the television and I was sold, no trial period needed. Cereal, toys, bubblegum, laundry detergent, it really didn't matter. I wanted it—or I wanted my mother to buy it. I can remember choosing sides between competitive products: was I a Crest girl or a Colgate girl? Pepsi or Coke? Downey or Snuggle? In my little bitty four-year-old mind, these decisions were important and they helped me organize and sort the big, grown-up world around me, helped me create an identity through the use of labels. I was a girl who liked Crest and Coke and Snuggle Fabric Softener, and I was most definitely *not* the girl who like Colgate, Pepsi, or Downey. Commercials showed me what life could be like if only I had . . . fill-in-the-blank product. I was every marketing firm's dream child. My mother, however, was impervious to such consumer-driven ploys, and seemed to live to thwart my ad-inspired desires. Until I discovered The Finger Paints. Watching the commercial for this most amazing product over and over during Saturday morning cartoons led to a mild obsession with getting my hands on my very own set of finger paints. The kids in the commercial seemed to have so much fun painting brightly colored rainbows and radiant-hued flowers with their pots of deep blues and rich reds. If there was a creative utopia for children, surely finger paints were at the center of it. Somehow, someway, I was determined to have my own set.

I can only imagine the lengths I must have gone to trying to convince my mother, the penny-pincher of all penny-pinchers, to buy me a set. I am sure there were musical numbers, picket-line posters, and perfectly timed nightly prayers all aimed at winning my case. My mother, frugal but not unfeeling, did what she could, scrimping and saving until she could buy me the very same set, the Name Brand Set I had seen in the commercials. Excited to share her gift, Mom set me up at the table, laid the Name Brand waxy paper out in front of me, and wrapped an old shirt of my father's around me. I watched as she carefully twisted off the lid of each pot of paint, staring into the gelatinous mounds of colors and then, once all the lids were safely removed, she gave me the okay. I enthusiastically began dipping my fingers into the pots of brilliant paints, each the consistency of day-old pudding. The story goes that within moments I pulled my fingers out, held them up, and with a look of horror on my face said, "Ewwwww! It's all sticky!" That was the end of my finger painting career and the last time my mother bought me a Name Brand item as seen on television.

Neither my love of slick advertisements nor my aversion to getting my hands dirty ended there. Lack of talent is not the only reason I am not a potter or sculptor. I believe body lotion is a necessary evil I must endure for the sake of my skin, and I only mix dumplings by hand because the payoff of fluffy hot dumplings in a bowl of broth is worth the few minutes of sensory discomfort I experience when my hands are completely coated in the sticky, wet dough. So, it should come as no surprise that digging in the dirt is something I could have lived the rest of my life without and not missed one bit.

And had it not been for The Awful Year, breaking my foot, Jeremiah 29:5, and The Rule of St. Benedict, I might never have dug in the dirt or planted a single flower. God, life, and the universe had other plans for me.

We needed to plant a garden, and I was going to have to help.

We noticed, after our disastrous first attempt, that any time the boys were in the yard helping Nathan, and I remained inside, before long the boys made their way back into the house, leaving Nathan working alone and frustrated. We also noticed that if I wasn't home, things went swimmingly. Nathan and the boys worked hard and well together. So, it seemed the variable in our success was the participation rate of those persons at home. If four people were home and only three people were working, then things were sure to go bust, but if three people were home and three people were working, then things would go well.

If we were ever going to fulfill key lessons of this whole experiment—planting gardens and eating what grows there, learning to thrive as a family, and working together in community—then it had to be an all-hands-on-deck endeavor. And because I was the one most likely to be found indoors instead of out, there was a big neon sign over my head that said Weakest Link.

As is true with every growth moment in my life, I had come to the place where I was ready to admit that the only thing I could change about the situation was my part in it. Sure, I wished the boys wanted to work in the yard for the joy of it, or that Nathan could delegate the chores more clearly, or that a master gardener would take on our yard as a lifelong project. But those things were (a) unrealistic and (b) completely out of my control. The only things I could change were my actions and my attitude. This meant I was going to have to learn to work outside.

Along with getting my hands dirty, I also am not drawn to plants and earth the way I am drawn to livestock and paint chips. Nathan has the green thumb, not me. Given the choice, I would rather spend a Saturday morning wandering around a flea market than a plant nursery. When we go to the feed store, I head straight for the baby chicks or the galvanized tub display, daydreaming about cute blog posts and party themes. Looking at the supplies to turn our backyard into a viable garden, all I saw was itchy legs, a sore back, stiff knees, and crusty hands. When I imagined the fields at my dream farm, I was walking through them having deep thoughts, picking fruit off existing trees, and cutting down my own Christmas tree in the woods. I was raising goats and sheep and chickens, and helping Nathan build cute coops and pens as darling as a vintage Fisher-Price play set.

But hoeing, tilling, planting, and weeding all those open acres? No thank you. I would leave all of that to Nathan. Maybe the harvesting. I might help with the harvesting. You can carry a cute basket, and wear a great floppy hat, and Instagram the heck out of the fruit of your (or in my case, my husband's) labors. I just wanted to get on the farm, remodel the tiny house, and set about blogging about my wonderful new country life.

"No one is excused from rendering service to others. No one is exempt from performing the mundane tasks of daily life," John McQuiston II wrote in his modern interpretation of The Rule of St. Benedict. The mistake I had been making for years was excusing myself from *performing the mundane task of daily life* called yard work, thinking myself exempt from rendering help to Nathan in this area of our life. Because of this, my children also saw themselves as exempt. Yard work was equal to "Daddoe's work" in their eyes, a lesson they had learned, unfortunately, from me.

To plant gardens is one of the directions given to the Israelites during their exile, and it is one of the directions given to me as I tried to find a new way to live, a slower way, a more whole way—to help me be present to my life as it was. We needed to reclaim our tiny plot of land, following the wisdom stitched on pillows everywhere: we need to bloom right where we are planted. But before I led our family into another yard work disaster, I decided I should start with myself. I would try and learn how to dig in the dirt.

I began by creating new Pinterest boards filled with pictures of English gardens and flower patches. I added gardening blogs to my feed reader, I made cute garden stakes out of clothespins, I bought a new straw hat, I daydreamed about hosting a big farm-to-table-style dinner on our back patio for all our friends. But still, no dirt. I was no closer to having a garden or knowing how to work in the yard as a family than I had been in the summer.

A few years earlier, for Christmas, my parents had given my siblings and me organic gardening kits, complete with heirloom seeds, potting soil, and fertilizer. The entire package had sat in a plastic bin in the back of our laundry room gathering dust as I saved those seeds for our someday farm. But the time had come to break out the seeds, and out of my fantasy. Over Easter weekend I sat at the kitchen table with my Aunt Teija and let her walk me through how to start plants from seeds. One by one I planted itty bitty tomato seeds in empty egg crates. Pressing the seeds into a mixture of fertilizer and dirt and water, my fingernails became black, the dirt crusting over my fingertips. That evening two egg crates of pole bean, tomato, and okra seeds rode home with me in the front seat. Once at home, I placed them on the kitchen table by the window, whispering "grow, please," as I watered them one more time. After days, maybe even weeks, of watering and rotating the crates in front of the window, little sprouts began to break through the surface.

I don't do a whole lot of things that I am bad at. It's my way of preventing embarrassment and shame. I hate to be corrected. I hate to be corrected so much that I have come up with two defense mechanisms. First, I don't try new or hard things in public. Then if it can't be avoided, I announce how terrible I am at something before I try it. I set the bar really low in advance, and I laugh about how awful I will be. I talk about how I love mess and authenticity and going slow, and how great it is to embrace all our flaws (I do believe that wholeheartedly). But sometimes I twist these words, using them for less-than-authentic reasons. I do this a lot when I am feeling particularly messy and flawed about something that feels itchy and tinged with childhood shame. Like being overweight, or being bad at grammar. It is just easier to pretend it is *who I am, y'all* and *like, I am so okay with it,* even when I'm not. When, truthfully, my heart is beating fast, my cheeks are flushed in embarrassment, and I am looking for the quickest escape route. I am ashamed and I am ashamed about how ashamed I am.

Shame loves to mock sincerity, loves to prove all your insecurities right, loves to remind you just how fake you really are. To put a protective buffer between what Anne Lamott calls Bad Mind and myself, between shame and myself, I declare that I love many of the things I actually hate about myself; I go ahead and pull the rug out from under myself, making myself look like a lovable goof, instead of the complete failure I know myself to be. In high school this protective buffer would have been my disdain of cheerleaders. "Oh look, they are so fake and false and snobby; I am so glad I am not one of them," I would have said on the outside, while on the inside I would have given anything to have their athletic talent, their shiny hair, their flat stomachs, their easy way of walking through the halls.

I realize now this is false humility. It smacks of arrogance and image control. I see it in my children: this unwillingness to look foolish, to be silly, to risk. I have passed this trait down to them both in different ways, and I am not proud of it. With my words I tell them, "Don't be afraid to ask questions. Don't be afraid to try things you aren't already great at." But then, do they ever see me do these things? Do I ever take a true risk in broad view of everyone?

Losing the sale of our house and consequently the farm was brutal on my ego. I had failed at producing my dream-come-true ending. Not only for myself but for my blog readers. The day the buyers backed out of the deal, I lay in bed crying huge, heaving sobs. Along with the constant *Why?* I gasped two questions: *How will we tell the boys? And how will I tell my readers?*

The first question was legitimate, though in retrospect I realize (and perhaps I knew this in the moment) I was projecting my own all-consuming sadness onto them. They were disappointed, yes, but they quickly rejoiced at getting to stay in the only home they had ever known a little longer and moved on to the next question—did this mean we could get more chickens?

The second question was ridiculous. It only served to highlight the awful, brutal truth I had desperately tried to ignore. My motives for wanting to change my life had become a convoluted mess. My ego and my pride were so wrapped up in this plan.

Needing new blog fodder is no reason to change your whole life, unless perhaps this is how you make your living. Wanting to be as popular as other bloggers who live on farms is a sad, junior-high type of motive. Wanting to be cool is a hideous state to be in; it is embarrassing because, frankly, I should be too cool to want to be cool. I should be above cool. But even this train of thought is all arrogance and shadow throwing.

The truth is, cool shouldn't matter. I shouldn't be above it, or below it, or next to it, or in it. Cool shouldn't even be on my radar. But I am human, you are human, and cool is something we all struggle with on some level. Since Adam and Eve put fig leaves on, humans have been worried about image control. Since Cain and Abel brought different offerings, humans have been worried about who is In and who is Out. Since Isaac and Ishmael, the race has been on to see who is loved more. And all our insecurities spread like weeds under the grow lights of competition and pride.

I don't know about you, but my entire bathroom vanity and wardrobe is filled with things meant to help me hide my flaws. From a product actually called *concealer* to the modern-day torture-device-like versions of the corset meant to restrict, pull, tuck, and hide any flaw around my middle, I have employed a wide variety of gadgets to hide what I see as my outward flaws. And that's only my physical appearance. I hide flaws all over the place—from the well-curated Instagram post, where the mess is cropped out and the lighting is just right, to the closet I stuff full of all the odds and ends when company comes over. I hide or deflect my flaws, real and perceived, all the time. And I don't do things I stink at. Like gardening. I sure don't put my inabilities on display. I absolutely don't ask someone better than myself—someone who can see through my false self—for help.

But if I were going to learn how to put down actual, tangible roots, if I were going to model all the things I said I believed in—humility, grace, vulnerability, community, sweat equity, and stability—if I were going to live from a place of wholeness and authenticity instead of false humility and bravado, I would need help. I would need to transfer my fragile little seedlings into the earth and begin a garden.

A core value of the Benedictine way of life is Mutual Obedience; it involves *consulting others, seeking advice, expressing desires, giving feedback, inviting initiative— all for the common good.* By opening myself up to seek advice from Nathan, by consulting him and sharing my weakness with him, I would be helping myself, and my family, thrive where we are. So, one lovely spring morning, spade in hand, gathering my duel reserves of humility and courage, I asked Nathan to help me learn how to garden. I asked him to show me how to turn over the ground, how to make a place for each and every pod, how to clear the dirt of weeds and grass, and how to add little bits of worm compost to the soil.

We began by planting pole beans in the little area at the end of the patio, underneath an iron arch I had found on the side of the road, where they could grow up tall and supported. Inspired by this small bit of progress on my part, Nathan and the boys turned over a plot of land and began to clear the vines covering the fences, throwing all the bits into the chicken run where Rosie, the queen of the roost, would jump on top of the pile and cluck her ownership for all to hear.

Over the next week we planted the tomatoes I had started Easter weekend. The following weekend we bought squash plants at the feed store and planted them by the tomatoes. We bought a tiny white picket fence and put it around our garden to keep out our huge white farm dog. When that didn't work, I made a garden bunting out of vinyl tablecloths and twine, hanging it above the fencing. What it lacked in functionality, it more than made up for in cuteness.

Over the course of that spring and summer, I worked hard to stay involved in the reclaiming of our yard. I went to the gardening stores with Nathan. I planted soybeans and staked the tomatoes. I sweated and cursed, bent my back out of whack, and was present. Working as a family, Nathan taught the boys and me how to lay pavers, rake leaves, weed-eat the walkway, and lay mulch in the flower beds. We worked together as a team, as a family, to be better stewards of our property. And we waited for our plants to bloom as we entered into the slowness that is the growing season. Time and time again it seems I have to learn that *most growth takes time*. Yes, it can happen fast, like a weed shooting up, or a teenage boy's growth spurt, or a baby girl cutting teeth. Sudden traumatic events in our lives—birth, death, loss, betrayal—these things can cause quick growth as well. But these are anomalies, and thank goodness, because fast growth is painful and gut-wrenching.

Most growth, the everyday kind, is so slow that it is almost imperceptible. It also requires a lot of daily maintenance. Pulling weeds, clearing out debris, watering, tending, feeding. These chores can be meditative, and they can be a pain, but they have to be done whether you are in the mood or not. In my experiment of being at home in this life, I was learning how to live at a slower, more intentional pace. And, digging into the life I had, working to cultivate wholeness in the process, I had to show up daily and try, try, again. I had to do things I didn't feel like doing in order to honor the call to be a better steward of all I had been given, to be a faithful caretaker of my life and family, to grow in my love for God and others. And it wasn't just me doing the dirty work. That spring, we all showed up and did things we didn't want to do. Nathan slowed down and worked to teach each of us how to use tools and pull weeds. I put down my computer and put my hands in the earth, letting them get caked and sticky with compost and dirt. The boys got in there with us and found their strides, embracing every motorized tool they were allowed to use.

When summer arrived we rejoiced in our smallest success stories. We managed to harvest a dozen tomatoes, a handful of beans, and a few crooked-neck yellow squash, but bunnies and bugs and our dog, Maizey, demolished the rest. It wasn't Pinterest-worthy but it was ours.

Together we had tackled the direction to dig in, serve each other, thrive. And at the end of the summer we ate the last surviving squash and sliced huge beefsteak tomatoes to go with our steak and grits and celebrated that we at long last had done what we set out to do all those months ago. We had planted a garden and eaten what grew there, and together, as a family we had thrived.

chapter 13

Conversion: Lessons from a Worm Farm

There are more failures because of the use of fresh manure than from any other cause. It is an excellent material if properly rotted and composted, but the touch of fresh manure means death to many a bulb.
—*The Complete Book of Garden Magic* by Roy E. Biles

Conversion is not the smooth, easy-going process some men seem to think. . . . It is wounding work, this breaking of the hearts, but without wounding there is no saving. . . . Where there is grafting there will always be a cutting, the graft must be let in with a wound; to stick it onto the outside or to tie it on with a string would be of no use. Heart must be set to heart and back to back or there will be no sap from root to branch. And this, I say, must be done by a wound, by a cut.
—John Bunyan

There is so much I have left to learn about gardening, but this I know: every spring the garden must be dug up and turned over. The earth must be tilled, broken up, and prepared by adding in disgusting, smelly compost—the manure, the waste, from our worms.

Upon reflection it occurs to me that I may want to be more specific in my prayers, because that summer—the one of The Awful Year—we did get a farm at long last; we actually inherited one from my grandfather. Only it wasn't the kind of farm that comes with twenty acres and a house. We ended up with a worm farm. Yep. A worm farm. It's a real thing, y'all.

A worm farm is a small, multistory complex; worm farms come in a variety of shapes and sizes, and can be handmade or ordered from your favorite worm farm catalog. My grandfather had ordered the worm farm we inherited from a catalog in the late 1980s, and it came all the way from New Zealand. Before he ordered the farm, he kept his worms in a simple wood box he made himself out of scraps. The box lived in the dark, damp space under the kitchen sink, where he could easily toss scraps from the day's meals—the orange peels, the carrot tops, the pepper seeds—to feed his worms. But at some point, perhaps after the first harvest of castings, my grandmother said, "that's enough, dear," and the worms were banished to live and work all their days outside in the new condoplex. From a distance this "farm" looks like four tires stacked on top of each other, resting on short stilts. Up close you can see that it is actually four round plastic trays, each about the width of a tire but not as deep, with tiny holes into which we throw leftover uncooked kitchen scraps for the worms to eat. Each tray has a function in the decomposition process, and the goal is that together they will produce a rich compost made of worm castings, and a dark brown liquid called Worm Tea (a fancy way of saying worm pee). Both of these things—the compost and the tea—are a wonderful gift for our garden as they are loaded with nutrients and vitamins—and all sorts of other amazing things well-composted manures carry.

Surprisingly (at least to me), there is a wealth of spiritual wisdom to be found in running a worm farm. I have read whole books that have taught me wonderful truths, but I could have saved my pennies had I paid better attention to our little Red Wigglers. But then, a worm farm isn't really something you want to spend a lot of time staring at, especially when there is a fresh batch of grub worms, which, let's just be honest, are gross to look at (my apologies to the Creator). And yet, there are the lessons, hidden deep in what is trash and poop.

Lesson 1: Worms are conversion experts.

Conversion, in the Benedictine tradition, is more than a brief moment of confession or belief. St. Benedict understood it to be a lifelong process, a never-ending stretching of the soul, resulting in being changed from glory to glory. But we must be willing—isn't that always the rub?—to give ourselves over to this process of being refined and changed daily. We must choose time and time again to turn away from our own agendas, and reorient ourselves to Christ's agenda: to love God and love our neighbors—our families, our coworkers, our trash collectors, our leaders, and our enemies—as ourselves. Conversion is transformation, and transformation is never painless.

Leftover onion skins, celery leaves, the peels of potatoes, acorn squash long forgotten and abandoned in the back of the refrigerator: these things that are usually tossed in the trash or pushed down a garbage disposal, unusable by themselves, are the beginnings of what will nurture growth in our garden. The conversion of scraps and trash by the worms into dark, rich, life-giving fertilizer is an ongoing process. In winter, it can take weeks for our worms to completely eat a large piece of cabbage or a rotten cucumber. In the summer months, the worms are so active that we can't keep them fed to satisfaction. But whatever the season, they work at their own pace. Worms should be the mascot for Slow Living.

For years, I was prey to the New Notebook Syndrome. You know the one. It tells you that if you go ahead and buy an amazing new planner or journal, this will be the year you figure it all out—make sense of your life, your dreams, your challenges. Or maybe for you it is the new self-help bestseller, or the latest diet fad, or the newest tech gadget. We all have these things we cling to in the hopes that we will find the magic key to unlock all our disparate parts. For me it was journals. Beautiful blank journals. And then later planners. Each one filled with fresh, clean, unmarked, unspoiled pages with plenty of room to write of all the things that would be different this time. There is a running joke in my family along these lines. For years, at the beginning of her spring cleaning frenzy, my grandmother would declare, "This year we are going to get organized!" She is in her nineties and she is still trying to decide the most efficient way to organize her kitchen. Still searching for the key. But the truth is there is no key. There is no magic book, or diet, or device, or journal, or organization system from The Container Store that will create wholeness in me or you. Because growth doesn't happen that way.

This is the same lesson I was learning as we dug into our life: moving to a farm wouldn't bring about wholeness in me. No matter how much I wanted to believe otherwise, I knew deep down that what my mother said was unavoidably true: "You take you wherever you go." Ultimately my problem was not my house, my job, or my marriage. My problem was me, and only a Conversion of life, a Transformation of spirit and heart would help.

For me the conversion process—this learning to live slower, to be rooted and present—meant turning the "scraps and trash" of the life I didn't want into something new. I was going to have to open myself up to and participate willingly in reframing the story of my life.

No one longs for what he or she already has, and yet the accumulated insight of those wise about the spiritual life suggests that the reason so many of us cannot see the red X that marks the spot is because we are standing on it. The treasure we seek requires no lengthy expedition, no expensive equipment, no superior aptitude or special company. All we lack is the willingness to imagine that we already have everything we need. The only thing missing is our consent to be where we are.

—Barbara Brown Taylor

The Benedictine vows of Stability, Conversion, and Obedience are meant to help you notice the X beneath your feet. To help you give your consent to be where you are, noticing perhaps for the first time that the grass is green right here, wherever that is. So, like the worms, I would have to stay where I was, and do the work in front, underneath, and all around me, learning as I went.

Lesson 2: We all have to do our own work.

Despite their slimy appearance, worms are a wonderful and necessary part of the circle of life. In addition to being part of the food chain (birds and fish in particular are grateful for their presence), worms have important jobs in the ecosystems all around us. Earthworms help aerate the earth, and composting worms help create the fertilizer we use to grow robust, healthy food in our garden. These invertebrates are diligent workers, always moving, wiggling, eating, and tunneling. From what I can tell, a worm does not sit next to carrot skins and hope it will absorb the nutrients through osmosis. It does not wait for another worm to show up and make its tunnels for it; it doesn't skip a shift and hope someone else will pick up the slack. I have never seen a worm stop working because it doesn't like the work it has been given to do or because it doesn't feel like it. No matter how big a job is set before it, a worm just keeps on working, because that is what worms do.

Watching our little bitty worms go to town on a huge, disgusting, rotting pile of cabbage leaves, coffee grounds, and onion skins, it occurred to me that internalizing the practices of slowing down was not going to be a quick process. I couldn't read a book, say some prayers, have some deep thoughts, and call it a day. I would have to keep doing the work set in front of me, cultivating contentment one bite at a time. A highly inconvenient prospect, considering it might take me the rest of my life to complete it and I desperately wanted to be content yesterday.

Taking the vow of Conversion is a fancy monastic way of saying: I now agree to cooperate with God in my own transformation, doing the work set in front of me. Sometimes in the transformation process we get to change the things we don't like, and sometimes we only get to do as Maya Angelou suggested and change the way we think about them, but regardless, the work remains solidly in our court.

In Jeremiah, God instructs the Israelites to get busy making themselves at home, telling them to build houses and plant gardens and raise children. Nowhere in chapter 29 does God say, *Hey, why don't you lie around some more and whine? You will be so much happier if you do. No,* God says, *get to work, dig in, adjust your thinking.* Which is also what God was saying to me.

"There is no limit to the ways in which God may bring us to our senses, making us aware that it is time, and past time, to get on with it, to turn back, to the paths of righteousness," writes Kathleen Norris in *Amazing Grace.* My worms get on with their transforming work with no need for awakenings or aha moments, but I, a sentient being, continue to get stuck, lost, and turned around, confused by the desire for an easy path, a clearer solution, a pain-free existence. I once heard a preacher say, "God loves you just as you are, but God also loves you too much to leave you that way." I think maybe there is a whole lot of good and bad theology mixed up in this statement; implications of force and manipulation could be extrapolated if one were tempted to believe God to be a great puppet master in the sky. But there is something good in there about conversion. It hints at the idea that God wants to partner with us in our growth, that God's love is a cooperative love—rooting for us and not against us. Maybe the more correct version would be something along these lines: *God loves us just as we are, just as we were, and just as we will be, and anytime we are ready to do transforming work, God is loving us there as well.*

Lesson 3: Community is our spiritual gizzard.

The gizzard is the part of the worm that breaks down the last of the worm's dinner, preparing it for digestion. One of my favorite kitchen gadgets is a vintage nut grinder. If you have never seen one of these amazing contraptions, run to your local flea market and find one. They are wonders for chopping nuts and keeping kids occupied in the kitchen. Mine is vintage circa 1960s and is aqua blue, as are most things in my kitchen. (I might have an addiction.) Anyway, there is a small metal or plastic cup called the hopper, which sits on top of a glass jar of some shape. At the bottom of the hopper is a metal grinder and a hand crank. You pour your nuts into the hopper, set to turning the crank and—voila!—little bits of nut appear in the jar below. This is similar to how a gizzard works. The gizzard's job is to break down the worm's food so it can be easily digested and absorbed. Gizzards are tough, muscular, and sometimes filled with tiny stones that aid in breaking down the matter. The gizzard is the refining fire of the worm's gut, and living community is the gizzard of the Conversion process.

As with sweat-inducing, muscle-stretching hard work, refining fire is necessary, and there is no replacing it. There is no substitute. When we remain in a place believing God will use both the location and the people in that place to grow us, we are practicing Stability, and it is in the midst of this practice that conversion begins to happen. In doing life with other humans, by choice or by chance, God begins to grind up our assumptions—about ourselves, the nature of sin, who does or doesn't deserve forgiveness, and what our lives should or shouldn't be about. During this season of learning how to slow down and dig, of being committed to both the place where I lived and the people I lived with, my own spiritual gizzard got a workout.

Before everything went topsy-turvy, before the dog died and the chickens were killed and the house sale fell through, in the brief window of time when Nathan and I thought we would be moving to a farm, we each daydreamed about what life would be like once we moved, and how to improve on the little homestead we had found.

Most of my daydreams centered around turning the little shack of a house into the cutest fixer-upper of all time, gutting the tiny kitchen, replacing flooring throughout the house, installing shiplap on all the walls. The little bitty house would be a challenge, yes, but it was a challenge I was excited to tackle in exchange for moving to a farm. But it wasn't only the house I was excited about. I was also excited about the outdoor space and buildings—specifically the barn and the small hill behind it.

The barn was not huge, but what it lacked in size it made up for in charm. The well-worn structure had exposed rafters in the ceiling, concrete floors, and wooden plank walls. At each end, huge barn doors rolled open, creating a great pass-through down the middle of the structure; as soon as I looked at it I knew it was the perfect party space. Soon I was imagining strands of twinkling lights hanging from the exposed beams, a large narrow farm table surrounded by mismatched wooden chairs at one end, and a dance floor at the other. And everywhere I saw Mason jars and coffee cans filled to the hilt with the wildflowers I would grow on the little hill behind the barn. This hill was the one place on the farm I wanted as my own, to be my personal meditation area, a place where I could walk and think at the end of the day, running my hands through the flowers as I let all the worries and stresses float away. A place where I could take an old quilt and hide in the tall grasses, lying on my back, staring at the clouds, listening to the birds and the breeze.

One would think that in the year and a half we spent trying to buy the property, we would've discussed our plans for the twenty acres and various outbuildings. That we would have carefully and thoughtfully worked together, making sure we were on the same page of expectations and dreams before we even made an offer.

But one would be wrong.

It wasn't until the month leading up to the purchase of the farm that I mentioned my meditation hill and party barn plans to Nathan, plans that he immediately rebuffed as he lay out his agenda for working the hill for crops. Nathan—a person who found spiritual healing in digging, planting, and harvesting—imagined standing at the foot of that little hill with rows and rows of purple hull peas, Arkansas tomatoes, and heaps of peppers and cabbage. He saw the chance to find meaning, wholeness, and the satisfaction that comes from getting your hands into the earth. And in his mind's eye, the garden would conveniently be right next to the barn, a barn he imagined would be filled with his someday tractor, rakes and shovels, tillers, and all the other farming implements he could gather, along with a small wood shop at one end.

As it turned out, we had both staked a lot on that hill—both of us saw the hill as part of our personal restoration story, and the barn as a place to house what we each loved best—for me, gathering people together; for him, working with his hands. And neither of us was willing to budge on our plans. This discovery led to one of those monumental fights that will live forever in infamy. The fight was so large, the tears so great, the bitterness so cutting, that we took our issue straight to our marriage therapist, who of course refused to pick sides, but did ask one particularly interesting set of questions.

As Nathan and I sat at opposite ends of the sofa in his office, tears streaming down my face, our therapist asked us: Would you want this farm if you weren't married? Would you want to go for it alone?

I don't remember if we answered directly that day or not, but I know these questions changed the trajectory of our lives in many ways. They became our gizzard for the next two years. My answer was clear. No. I wouldn't want the farm if I weren't married to Nathan; I wouldn't want to carry it alone. Having the farm without him would be no good. For one, it would be too much work on my own—what did I know about plowing and reaping? Also, I knew how much joy moving to the country would bring him, how much wholeness and peace. One of the motivating factors in my desire to move was his happiness. I am not sure I would have even considered rural life if I weren't married to Nathan, so no, I wouldn't want a farm without him by my side.

Nathan's answer was the same—having a farm, living a country life, was something he had come to want only in the context of our relationship and life together. This idea, this desire, had never been his dream or my dream; instead, it had always been *our* dream.

Two weeks after our therapist posed these questions to us, the sale of our house fell through. There would be no moving anytime in the near future, no hill to fight over, no barn to disagree about. But the questions remained: Why did we want a farm anyway? For the quiet? For the party space? For the possible income? Did we want to move simply because it was easier than staying? Or, were we moving because we felt it was what we were meant to do?

It was more than obvious that our relationship needed a little tender, loving, and brutally beautiful—what Glennon Melton calls "brutiful"—care. We needed to learn to listen better, fight harder; we needed to learn to remain open and really hear the other person's heart behind the words. We needed to be vulnerable and courageous in our love and heap dose after dose of grace upon ourselves and each other. We needed to learn how to honor each other's dreams and desires, but more importantly, we needed to do some dreaming together. We needed to figure out where we wanted to live, but also how we wanted to live.

This is how we began to open ourselves up to the work of transformation within our family and our marriage. Over the next eighteen months there was a lot of refining-fire conversation—a lot of coming around again and again to the question: what do we really want our life to be like? There were mistakes and hurt feelings and aha moments and high fives. There were days we seemed to be writing the same story and days we seemed to be in completely different books. There were tears and ugly words; there was laughter and lovemaking. And over and over we returned to the one truth we knew: we didn't want to go it alone. We wanted to do it, whatever it was going to be—moving or staying—as a team. Corny as it sounds, we really are better together.

Lesson 4: Trust the leading of the Spirit.

Worms do not have eyes or ears; they are guided by their senses of light, movement, and vibration. Most of us are guided by a combination of hearing, sight, smell, feelings, and curiosity. For instance, we see things other people have and we want them. We hear how other people are praised and we want the same thing.

A feeling is aroused by a movie, a book, an interaction, and we want more of it. We are curious where the crowd is moving and we follow along. All day long we are flooded with images and words and sounds and status updates and tweets and blog posts. There is a nonstop barrage of opinion and persuasion and information flowing toward us, information we constantly sort and choose from, deciding what to like and what to unlike, what to accept and what to reject, what to take in and what to throw out. Worms don't have these sorts of options, choices, and challenges. Worms simply follow the streams of light and sensations of movement—vibrations from the earth and sky—and find their way.

My first understanding of the Holy Spirit was of a Jiminy Cricket sort of character: a good angel who sat on my shoulder and prompted me to tell my mother the truth, to wash my hands in the restroom, to not cheat off my classmate's paper. My second understanding was of the hankie-waving, tongues-speaking sort of Holy Spirit. I met this version in high school, when I attended revival meetings with my Pentecostal boyfriend. And while they seemed authentic, both seemed incomplete.

In *Traveling Mercies*, Anne Lamott tells about a sermon that her pastor gave one Sunday. Pastor Veronica talks of how, when she prays for guidance, a puddle of light will appear just beyond her feet. After she steps into it and stands there awhile, not knowing which way to go next, another small circle will appear, and so on and so forth, until she has traveled from puddle of light to puddle of light all the way to her destination. Reading Veronica's description, I am brought back to my worms and how they are completely guided by the light and vibration they sense happening around them, and I wonder if this is another picture of how the

Holy Spirit moves and leads. More than any other experience or explanation, this image of the Holy Spirit—as light, movement, and vibrations—resonates with me. Thinking in these terms, I can recall prayers, spoken and unspoken, where puddles of light, small streams peeking through cracks, glints, and glimmers reflecting off windows and mirrors shone through. I remember the stirrings in my soul, my heart, hairs standing up on my arms, a shift in the air, a change in plans, an awareness of Other. Unrest or contentment would bubble up, breaking through the surface of my consciousness, calling me to move, to go, to keep doing the work, to keep moving toward the light of love, toward wholeness.

We fed the worms kitchen scraps, taking them rotten tomatoes, withered grapes, and what seemed like a hundred corn husks, on into the fall months. When winter came, the worms slowed down their work, taking longer and longer to digest the apple cores and celery we threw out to them in the evenings. When spring came, and we again attempted to literally follow God's command to "plant gardens and eat what grows there," we dumped heaps of the worm compost onto our garden plot, mixing the dirt and the fertilizer together, until our entire garden was fortified with the rich nutrients from our worms' diligent labors.

We will all have mountaintop moments, times when we feel a great immediate shifting in our heart or life, when we find ourselves instantly changed, when our transformation from caterpillar to butterfly is swift and dramatic. But these are the exception and not the rule. The rule, instead, is this: transformation happens when we, like the worms, are willing to wiggle and move and squirm and work right where we are, as we are. We grow and change and evolve, most often, in the steady, daily act of showing up and doing the work in front of us: loving God, loving our neighbors, living our lives in communities we choose and communities we are assigned to, practicing authenticity, doing our best to be kindhearted, asking ourselves the hard questions about our motives, taking time to rest and play, and all the while turning back toward the light again and again, following movement and vibrations of the Spirit. These are the ways we change; this is how we grow. This is the lifelong process called Conversion.

How to Start a Worm Farm

Nathan's helpful suggestions:

1. Buy some worms
2. Put them in some dirt
3. Feed them scraps

My suggestion:

Go to ModernFarmer.com and search "Worm Farm."

PART 4

SPREADING OUT

chapter 14

Cooking, Listening, and Marriage

Wisdom is not gained by knowing what is right.
Wisdom is gained by practicing what is right, and
noticing what happens when that practice succeeds
and when it fails. Wise people do not have to be
certain what they believe before they act. They are
free to act, trusting that the practice itself will teach
them what they need to know.
—Barbara Brown Taylor

The willingness to show up changes us. It makes us a
little braver each time.
—Brené Brown

Nathan and I have always had a tumultuous relationship in the kitchen. When we first began dating, he was a banquet chef at a large state park lodge, and I was the girl who ate rice, cheese, and pineapple mixed together almost every night. To say his culinary experience was greater than mine would be an understatement. We are not unusual in the fact that we have one of *those* stories. You know the ones—the ones where one person cooks for the other person and everything goes wrong, flames and cursing and tears ruining whatever might be salvageable. My parents have a version of this story. It involves my mother trying to cook a folded steak in a toaster oven. This is how she tells it:

I had a counter cooker where I could bake things, it was a newfangled thing. Nana, your grandmother, brought some minute steaks to the apartment so that we would have something to eat after we got home from our honeymoon. I had never cooked a minute steak. In fact my mom didn't like us in the kitchen so we never really learned to cook (which explains a lot). I had not had fried food since my dad had had a heart attack when I was in grade school. So I thought I could cook the steaks in the little counter oven. I pulled them out to look at them and they fell on the floor. I did know not to waste anything, and I mean anything, so I picked them up and cleaned them off and put them back into the little oven. When I put them on the plate and tried to cut them they were like tough rubber. Your dad was not happy about that.

My parents were married in 1970, and this story has come up at least once a year ever since.

Our story of culinary disaster involves a loaf of bread, and really, how much trouble could one get into with a solitary loaf of Italian bread? Plenty.

With six people in our home, and one tight budget to work with, my mother did the best she could to keep our bellies full and our bodies clothed. We never went naked or hungry, but we also never had many of the little luxuries my friends had. For instance, we went decades without cable, we never had soda or potato chips in the house (unless my dad did the shopping that week), my parents never owned more than one car, and at times they didn't even own a car that could carry all of us at once. So I have never been sure if it is because of my mother's frugality or her lack of cooking panache, but I don't remember ever having had garlic toast at home. Buttered toast? Yes. Cheese toast? Absolutely! Garlic toast? Nope. We did, however, eat quite a bit of cinnamon toast, pieces of sandwich bread slathered with butter and coated with sugar and cinnamon, toasted under the oven broiler, the edges nice and crisp, the middle warm, melty with sweet buttery goodness—a poor man's substitute for cinnamon rolls.

The first time I cooked for Nathan I made something Italian—maybe spaghetti? Or fettucine Alfredo with sauce from a jar? I am not really sure. But I am confident that I chose the menu because I thought it would be romantic, like something out of a chick flick movie. Wanting to create a whole meal, I decided we should have garlic bread with our pasta and salad, but instead of broiling *slices* of French bread, I put the whole loaf in the oven on the top rack, with the broiler on, the same way we did with our cinnamon toast, and walked away.

While I was blissfully setting the table for two, trying my best to be domestic and romantic, I asked Nathan to please check on the bread. But instead of a warm loaf of garlic bread, what he pulled out of the oven was a mini-bonfire. The whole loaf was lit up, flames shooting out of the top like fireworks. He quickly put out the fire with a dish towel, and then laughing, turned to me and asked why in the world I would do such a thing. What nonsense would possess me to put it so close to a raging hot broiler? Mortified, confused, and defensive, my cheeks as red and as hot as the top of the bread, I explained how we always cooked our toast on "broil" growing up. To which my professional cook fiancé asked, "Did you cook the whole loaf that way? Or just the slices?" Realizing my mistake, I gulped back tears of embarrassment and shame. Not only had I spoiled the bread, but I had spoiled the image I had of myself as a capable cook and planner of romantic dinners. And worst of all, Nathan had seen through me—he had seen through my false bravado and grand plans, straight to the little girl who had grown up in a home where making do also quite often meant doing without.

I have always been a little sensitive about my family, about what they taught me and about what they didn't. In college, thrown into shared living quarters with strangers, I began to really realize how many wonderful things I had learned from our creative make-it-work home life (all my crafty skills for one). But there were many practical lessons I missed, like how to handle money, or heat up a whole loaf of bread.

My garlic bread experience with Nathan was the beginning of our issues in the kitchen—really it was the beginning of all the issues we have ever had collaborating. Unbeknownst to him, that night Nathan had touched a very tender and raw spot in my heart—a spot that always feels behind the crowd, always feels like an outsider, always feels small, always feels dumb. Because of this, I was reluctant to let him back in. The embarrassment I felt failing at something that should have been so obvious and so simple was too painful, and I couldn't risk it happening again. So I kept up the bravado, the can-do, make-do, you-aren't-the-boss-of-me attitude for the first fifteen years of our marriage in order to protect my heart, my ego, my self-image.

Nathan's approach to life is to learn how to do things perfectly, expertly, with precision. My approach is to jump in feet first and figure it out on the ground, as I go. Nathan loves manuals and instructions. I abhor them. I like to feel my way through a problem, researching solutions to challenges only when I encounter them. He likes to do his research on the front end, taking copious notes, watching YouTube video after YouTube video, making list after list, drawing diagrams and working out contingencies. I like to look at a few pictures, start the project, and then refer to Google when I get stuck.

This is not only how Nathan fixes the car's brakes or remodels our kitchen. This is also how he cooks. During our married life he has been through several culinary phases, but most notable were his Julia Child phase and his Bread Phase. The Julia Child phase included a full-on Julia invasion in our home. Videos, books, more books, out-of-print books, online articles, nightly viewings of her shows or interviews, the whole nine yards. Once he had absorbed all the details, all the information, then came the cooking. The rich, fragrant, mouthwatering cooking. Cooking that sometimes took hours or days—light, fluffy soufflés, thick juicy pots of coq au vin, hot bowls of French onion soup capped with thick slices of Swiss cheese. It was a delicious phase, but it was also all-consuming and I am not sure my waistline ever recovered. Following, but completely inspired by, the Julia phase came the Bread Phase. I have to admit I did love this phase more, although it was just as intense, if not more so. Whole weekends were planned around the rise and fall of bread dough. Alarms were set for 2 AM. There were bastings and turnings and pattings. Room had to be made in the refrigerator, various flours were tested, new pans had to be purchased. For those few months, a fine film of flour dust covered every inanimate object in our kitchen.

I cook largely by intuition, experimentation, and experience (don't put things like bread loaves close to the boiler). When trying something new, I casually glance at a few recipes and then go off on my own, throwing together what I think will work with what I read. I tend to get my inspiration from what we have on hand rather than a thought-out plan. Most of my meals are some sort of pasta dish or salad or pot pie, or a combination thereof, all created from whatever I can find at the last minute.

Because most of my ideas come to me as I work, without hard-and-fast recipes guiding me, I am generally making up the temperatures and timing as I go along. Even when I make a familiar meal or dish, I will often make substitutions or change the order of cooking and combining ingredients, feeling my way as I add and subtract. This makes it hard to bring someone else into the process, especially when that someone approaches cooking completely differently, from a right-way-and-wrong-way perspective and with directions and measuring spoons.

In Jeremiah 29, in God's instructions to the people of Israel on how to live a full life while in exile, one of the commands given is to marry (verse 6)—a way to encourage the Israelites to stop waiting for their "real life" back in Jerusalem to start, and get on with things. In my own sort of exile—living in a house I didn't want in a place I didn't want to be in—I was doing my best to follow the instructions in Jeremiah 29 with the hope that I would learn how to get on with the business of living. I wanted to stop running from where God had planted me, and instead grow roots of gratefulness and joy in the here and now. Since I was already married, I decided perhaps the best way to pursue this command was to work on staying married.

Learning to work cooperatively, submitting to mutual obedience: these are monastic values taught in the Rule of St. Benedict. The Latin root for the word *obedience* is *obaudire*, which means *to listen*, and this is how St. Benedict's Rule begins: *Listen carefully my son, to the master's instructions, and attend to them with the ear of your heart.*

Mutual Obedience is really mutual listening, going beyond the words, seeking to discover what is behind them. Obedience in the Benedictine tradition is seen as an "expression of love and acting of mutual responsibility." It is not about control. Instead, obedience is about how we listen and how we respond, the goal being to do so from a place of mutual respect, acceptance, tenderness, and trust.

As I thought about how we could work on our marriage, it seemed obvious that we needed to learn how to listen to each other with our hearts and not our egos. Perhaps one of the reasons we had failed at selling our house and moving to the farm was a lack of Mutual Obedience; we were not truly listening to each other, and we were not doing the work required to really hear what the other was trying to say.

This lack of listening was a big reason Nathan and I had never been able to collaborate in the kitchen without someone leaving mad and frustrated. But this wasn't the only reason we had trouble working as a team. Brené Brown writes this in *The Gifts of Imperfection*:

> We cultivate love when we allow our most vulnerable and powerful selves to be deeply seen and known, and when we honor the spiritual connection that grows from that offering with trust, respect, kindness and affection.

I am pretty sure she wrote this sentence specifically for me. When it came to working with Nathan on big life decisions or in the kitchen, I was not allowing my most vulnerable and most powerful self to be seen and known, which meant I was often defensive and resistant to any input he gave. I began to realize that when I cooked with him, I felt naked and exposed, my emotions raw before we even began. Because Nathan knows the perfect technique for things like cutting bread, sautéing mushrooms, dicing onions, and slicing a roast, I felt as if every glance was a criticism, every question he asked an attack. Again and again, I was thrown right back to a place where I felt small, wrong, and humiliated. But I had never told him these things. I had never confessed how his questions—even if he meant them innocently—made me feel. Instead I hid behind tears and a short fuse, and for a decade stayed out of the kitchen when he was in it.

One of the things I learned during The Awful Year was that one of Nathan's main love languages is Doing Things Together. Which, for the record, is not one of mine. At all. Where he would rather us walk around the grocery store together, getting all the things we need for the week, I would rather split the list and be in and out quicker. But Nathan gets energy and feels loved when we do things together—projects, chores, shopping, life. For the sake of this whole being-present-to-my-life experiment, following the instructions in Jeremiah and St. Benedict's Rule, I decided there was no better relational mountain to try and climb than learning how to work together in the kitchen, cooking a meal.

So we tried it. And it was, as it had always been, a disaster. I was upset, bruised, and resentful, and Nathan was confused and frustrated. We ate dinner without speaking to each other, focusing all our attention and words on the boys. But I refused to be defeated so soon. Nathan and I are mostly reasonable, mature, loving people. We wanted nothing but good things for each other. Surely there was a way that we could learn to do something as simple as making dinner together.

After the kids were tucked in, and all the evening chores were finished, we climbed into bed and began to unpack why this common, everyday thing was so hard for us. That night we began the practice of listening with our hearts instead of our egos, we slowed down, and we got honest. I began to allow myself to be vulnerable about why I always reacted so strongly to his questions and glances. I cracked the door open enough for him to see how I struggled with feeling less-than from old wounds, and showed him my well-developed armor, armor I had put on long before he came along. To his great credit Nathan did not laugh or tell me those feelings were silly or useless. Instead he listened to them, he respected them, and he began to see how his expert-knowledge approach to cooking and life could come across as critical and arrogant. He saw how sometimes letting me do it my way was healthier for us both than him trying to convince me to do it the "right" way; and I, in turn, learned that I could trust him not to mock or ridicule me if I asked for help. I learned there is no shame in saying, "Will you teach me?"

At the end of the night we came to a compromise, a way of working together in the kitchen that felt comfortable to us both. We designed a system of assigned roles, which we stuck to until we grew comfortable and confident enough to actually collaborate. One of us would be Head Chef and one of us would be Sous-Chef for each meal we prepared together. Head Chef would pick the meal, the ingredients, and the way of cooking (be it planned or intuitive). Head Chef would also have to be organized and prepared enough to give Sous-Chef directions and tasks. Head Chef could give Sous-Chef responsibility for complete dishes if they so choose. Neither one, at any time, could give unsolicited, "helpful" tips or advice, *unless* the kitchen was about to catch fire. Both would practice humility and listening by asking for advice and tips throughout the process, letting go of judgment and any defensiveness. This may seem a funny system to some people, but for us it has worked. Sometimes growth happens organically, and sometimes growth requires a lot of intentional attention. Neither way is best and both are necessary.

We have now been cooking this way in the kitchen for several years, and at long last we are finding that the distinction of Head Chef and Sous-Chef isn't always needed. Instead we have found a rhythm of trust, developed better listening ears, and learned to lean on each other's strengths as we stretch our comfort levels. We still falter from time to time. Communication breaks down when we are tired or stressed; we can fall back into old assumptions and bad habits. But more and more, we are catching ourselves before we have gone too far. We are backing away from the edge of blame and defensiveness, and walking back toward each other, following the trail of kindness, trust, and affection to a place of listening and Mutual Obedience.

Coconut Chicken Curry Pile-Up Recipe

This is a great meal for families full of picky eaters or for a large gathering with friends, because everyone can pitch in no matter their culinary skills or budget. When planning your cooking time, remember to factor in cooking your favorite rice. I love to serve this over sticky sushi rice, while some people prefer it over basmati.

Ingredients

For the curry:

1 pound boneless chicken breasts, cut into chunks

2 sweet Vidalia onions, cut into chunks

2 cans of coconut milk (look for cans around 14 oz.)

2 teaspoons curry powder

1 teaspoon garam masala

½ teaspoon cayenne powder

2 cloves garlic, minced

1 cup chicken stock

1 red bell pepper, cut into strips

1 heaping tablespoon cornstarch suspended in 3 tablespoons cool water

3 tablespoons olive oil

For the Toppings:

Crunchy chow mein noodles

Shredded cheese (we typically use
    a mixture of Colby, cheddar,
    and mozzarella)

Diced green onions

Pineapple tidbits

Chopped peanuts

Chopped cilantro

Salt and pepper

Sriracha sauce

Directions

Brown the chicken with oil in batches in a stainless sauté pan on medium-high heat, along with handfuls of the onions. Don't crowd the pan, don't worry about it sticking. About two minutes before finishing the last batch, toss in the garlic and spice powders. Set all of this aside in a bowl or on a platter while deglazing the pan with the stock and coconut milk. Scrape up all of the brown stuff that caramelized on the bottom of the pan into the sauce with a wire whisk as it starts to boil. Dump the chicken with collected juices and the red pepper strips into the sauce and stir with a wooden spoon or spatula. As it comes back to a boil, stir in the thoroughly dissolved cornstarch and water. Let it simmer, uncovered, 10–15 minutes.

Serve with sticky rice.

To assemble

Serve coconut curry over the rice, and allow guests to add toppings to their taste. I love to pile it all on, but my boys tend to stick to the pineapple, cheese, and peanuts. Nathan loves everything including the Sriracha sauce, which I confess to leaving off.

chapter 15

Humility, Prayer, and a Crazy-Quilt Pot Pie

The miracle is not to walk on water, but on the earth.
—Thich Nhat Hanh

Sometimes when you need to feel the all-embracing nature of God, paradoxically you need to hang out in the ordinariness, in daily ritual and comfort.
—Anne Lamott

An interpretation of St. Benedict's Twelve Steps to Humility:

1. Admit I am not the center of the universe

2. Examine my motives for my choices and desires

3. Accept my limitations

4. Practice patience and self-restraint

5. Do not conceal my flaws

6. Be content with the work and life I have

7. See myself as ordinary—I am neither worse nor better than others

8. Remain true

9. Release my judgment of others

10. Develop true empathy

11. Listen to those around me and reply with sincerity

12. Live a life rooted in gratitude not entitlement

It is a well-known fact that the weather can wreak havoc on any baking process no matter how talented the chef. Humidity, altitude, extreme temperatures—they are all foils to a baker's best-laid plans. A cake falls, dough crumbles, and bread cracks. These are the risks bakers take each and every time they begin the journey of mixing water, flour, salt, yeast, sugar. But lately Mother Nature isn't the only one wreaking havoc in my kitchen. Just as the weather outside wafts in below windowsills and rises from the floorboards, another force leaves its mark on my cookies and crust: the weather inside.

The storms that blow through my heart can be as fierce as any that turn the metal windmill in our front yard. It is quite apparent to me that my pastry, like my newborn babies, can tell when I am feeling anxious, frazzled, excited, mournful, or numb. Dumpling dough under my rolling pin often knows before I do whether I will laugh or cry before the night is over. Maybe it is by the temperature of my hands, the force of my stirring, or the salty tears falling into the mixing bowl that my true feelings are revealed. However it works, my doughs and mixtures seem to absorb all of the tension or peace I am feeling, whether I like it or not.

Due to unexpected plumbing repairs and a rather nice vacation, our bank account had waned, meaning on this night, instead of ordering Chinese take-out, I would need to make do with creating a dinner out of the mismatched contents of the pantry and freezer. Exhausted and frazzled after a long day at work—and an even longer season of trying to learn the lessons of Jeremiah and St. Benedict—I was happily surprised to see the needed ingredients in my refrigerator for a kitchen-sink version of chicken pot pie, a one-dish meal that would make everyone happy.

To begin, the crust. Using the same recipe I have for years, I set to rolling out one half on a well-floured countertop. Almost immediately the dough began to stick to the surface, to the rolling pin, to the knife, to my hands. No amount of flour or sweet talking would convince it to cooperate. The dough was coming apart in pieces. And I wasn't far behind.

I wonder now if the dough could feel in every roll of the pin how desperately I wanted to lie down on the cold kitchen floor and be rolled out myself. How terribly thin and stretched I felt. How sticky and uncooperative everything in my life seemed to be. And how guilty and ungrateful I felt for not being able to buck up better.

I had reached the middle months of trying to be at home in this life, and the whole slow living, be content, dig-in thing was wearing thin. So many days, I felt as if I were pushing a boulder up a never-ending mountain. I was ready to stop being sad; I wanted to no longer be angry or disappointed or jealous every time I saw a farm on Instagram. I wanted to be truly happy with where we were. And I was trying, I was really trying, but learning to live the vows of Stability, Conversion, and Obedience is a lot harder than reading about them. I felt that I was failing at this lesson—as if I would never reach any sort of peace and contentment in the life I had.

Back at the counter, fighting with my pie crust dough, I eventually gave up. "Fine. Be that way!" I said to the crust, as I started peeling haphazard pieces of dough off the counter and pressing them into the bottom of my butter-greased iron skillet.

"Who cares if you aren't perfect? Who cares if you are pieced together? What does it matter? You don't seem to care, so I don't care!" I muttered as I pieced and pressed and patched the dough, somehow managing to cover the entire bottom and sides of my pan with a thin buttery layer of patchwork pie crust. My crust had reached the fifth stage of humility—do not conceal your flaws—it seemed, but I was still having trouble with it. In fact, I think I had fallen down at least to rung three—accept my limitations—or perhaps even rung one—admit that I am not the center of the universe.

Mumbling and grumbling is how I was talking to my pie crust, and at the time it was also how I was talking to God most days.

Everyday talking is the way I have always prayed. It is intuitive for me. As a preacher's kid and now in ministry myself, prayer for me has always existed in a variety of forms. There is the prayer of the historical church—the prayers we pray together out loud: *Our Father who art in heaven,* we begin each and every Sunday.

There are the psalms we sing weekly at the Episcopal church our family attends, and the collects the priest prays over us. There are the prayers that fill ancient prayer books, and there are the prayers of those who pray the daily office and keep the divine hours (something I long to do more of, but always somehow forget). There are the fiery prayers of the Baptist evangelists and preachers that filled my childhood—loud and impassioned prayers, filled with tears and pleas for mercy. There are the bedtime prayers said with my mother each and every night until when, at the age of sixteen, I declared myself too old for such sentimentality. There are the prayers we said around the table as a family whether we were eating at home or in a restaurant. There is the sinner's prayer, said at many a youth conference and revival meeting, and there are the songs said in other tongues that filled the small prefabricated building of the Pentecostal church my high school boyfriend called home. There are specific genres of prayers—intercessions, petitions, and thanksgivings—said deliberately, corporately, and silently all around the world.

But then there is another way of praying—a way I have always prayed but never known the name of until recently. It is a type of prayer I can only compare to breathing; it is called Practicing the Presence of God. Brother Lawrence, a seventeenth-century French lay brother, describes it as "a habitual, silent, and secret conversation of the soul with God." I do not know if I pray this way as a result of a childhood conviction that God is always with me, or my evangelical upbringing, or something written into my genetic code, but the truth of the matter is this: I talk to God all day long. God is ever-present with me. I cannot distinguish whether I feel it is God the Father, God the Son, or God the Holy Spirit with whom I am communing. Stemming from my childhood, the certainty continues that they are one in three and three in one, so what one knows the others know. So, I have never given much thought as to who was actually listening. In fact, I have long assumed they have tag-teamed this job of being with me for the past forty-odd years—comfort, mercy, wisdom, each showing up as needed.

This does not mean I walk around blissed out with goose bumps on my flesh all day, or that my prayers are answered more positively or quickly than anyone else's. Trust me: sometimes I feel as if perhaps the opposite is true, because God is so over me and all my talking—as if I am an annoying little sidekick who babbles on and on about each and every thing that pops into her head. But I do always have the sense that God hears, sees, and feels, and knows everything I see, hear, and feel, and therefore I talk to him much the same way I talk to myself. I pick up the conversation mid-thought; I talk out loud to him in the middle of the grocery aisle, and while I am driving, and when I am rummaging through thrift-store bins of cast-off silverware. I am the lady you see mumbling to herself in the dollar store and at Starbucks.

Of course there are days, even weeks, when I do not aim one intentional thought at God, times when I go silent as I work through something too hard even to name. But almost always, there is an awareness that because God is experiencing exactly what I am experiencing, we are together even in this silence. We are not lost to each other. The Spirit is there, waiting for me to find my words, when I am ready. And when I am ready, God will already know the backstory. I will not have to explain how I arrived where I am.

"Yes, when you get serious about finding me and want it more than anything else, I'll make sure you won't be disappointed," God says to the whining, unhappy, ungrateful Israelites. In those figuring-out times, I have the feeling the Holy Spirit is also saying this to me. *Are you ready to really find me? To stop your bitching and moaning and get on with your life? Are you ready to let me do a new work in you? If so, you will need to let me back in; you need to talk to me.*

This is the place I found myself in that day with the piecrust. I was coming out the other side of a prolonged silence, and the words I was sputtering angrily at the dough were a bit displaced. The truth is, these mutterings and sputterings were meant for God, and for myself.

Once the bottom crust was finished, I tossed in the filling mixture and poured chicken stock over it. I went back to the remaining dough, took a deep cleansing breath, and began to roll out the crust again as best I could, hoping to make a pretty top for my pie. But of course it fell apart, too. It was time to admit the limitations of my crust and of me: there would be no hiding the imperfect bottom crust with a perfect top layer. This crust was what it was.

So again, I patchworked it. I peeled the dough off the countertop and rolling pin piece by piece using a table knife. I covered the hodgepodge filling one patch at a time, until not a bit could be seen. It was only then that I remembered to preheat the oven.

It was then, waiting for my oven to heat, staring at a thrown-together meal, that I thought of Mark's account of those infamous loaves and fishes. The story goes like this: After a busy few days of healing and speaking and listening to the woes of the people, Jesus and his disciples head off for a mini-break. Word gets around of their destination and a crowd is waiting for them. Christ, not able to ignore the needs of the people, begins to teach. The disciples, forever taking care of their own agenda, are watching the clock. Before too long they give Jesus the "let's go" signal, but Jesus isn't quite done. So the disciples decide to try another tactic: concern for others. *Surely you are hungry, Lord. Surely the people are hungry. Let's go so they have time to grab dinner on the way home.* But Christ isn't buying it. He is onto them.

I have a better idea, he says. *Why don't you make dinner for everyone?*

The disciples balk. They were always balking at Christ's instructions. (Why am I always amazed by their ignorance, arrogance, and pure thickheaded ways? Why do I judge them so harshly? I am no better. I balk at Christ's call daily.) *But it's a budget buster!* they say. *The store is too far!* they complain. *Do we have to?* they whine.

Figure it out, he says. And so they do.

I am forever bumping up against reminders of why God is God and I am not. (You would think it was always obvious, but somehow I keep forgetting. I think it has something to do with being the eldest of four kids. Superiority complex and all that.)

What happens after the mass picnic is another one of these moments. After everyone's bellies are full and all the leftovers have been collected, Jesus sends the disciples on to their campsite while he wraps things up. This is no "Elvis has left the building" scenario; it is the opposite. Jesus stays until the last of the crowd has left, perhaps until the last lost toddler sandal has been found, the last lonely extrovert has finally stopped talking, and all physical traces of the picnic have been cleared. It is then that Christ leaves and goes off to pray alone before joining the others. This, to me, is grace.

If I were Christ, I would have been so put out with the disciples' knuckleheaded ways, I would have just left them to handle the crowd and the lost toddler shoes and the awkward talkative guy and taken a nice peaceful nap. Alone.

St. Benedict's twelve rules to live a traditional monastic life that began this chapter all point toward the eradication of pride and the practice of humility in its place. But without grace, even the pursuit of humility can become a race to win, a badge to earn, a trophy to place on the mantle, a way to keep the focus on me. Am I being selfless enough? Am I following the rules well enough? Am I serving enough? The focus is always on what I am doing—or not doing. But striving toward humility is still striving.

The oven is finally hot enough, and I put the pot pie in to cook. Once the middle is bubbly and the crazy-quilt crust is golden, I will leave it on the counter to rest for at least fifteen minutes before cutting into it. This resting and waiting is always the hardest part of pie making. The temptation to just dig into its steamy middle is strong, but the reward for waiting until the juices and the filling have set up is more than worth it. The fifteen minutes pass and I call everyone to the table. We all stare at our plates, a bit skeptical, until Nathan takes the first bite. His smile is all the encouragement we need. We dig in. The crust is perfect and flaky, each little piece its own bite of buttery goodness. Inside, the filling is thick and fragrant and hearty. The juices and flavors hold together, warm, rich, and comforting. We each eat crazy-quilt pot pie until our belly can't hold any more, grateful that we had used what we had, meager as it was, because in the end what we have is more than good. It is a gift. Nathan likes to say, "God will meet us wherever we are. *Wherever.*" That night, God met me in the midst of a messy, accidental meal. The Almighty heard my angry, frustrated words, and answered them with humility, warmth, and a full belly.

Forget about trying to win the badge of Most Humble; Benedict's Twelve Steps to Humility begin by reminding us to forget about ourselves and what we deserve or don't deserve, where we are or where we are not, and instead to respond always from a place of grace. The root of humility is grace, and grace is Christ. It is Christ becoming human and living human and dying human, by choice, for us. Nothing we can do, or not do, can earn us this grace. It is freely given, and our response to this impossibly generous, extravagant grace is the place where humility is born. For humility is all about honesty, honesty about who we are—the good, the bad, the embarrassing—where we are, and how we got here. Humility is not about thinking we are lower than others; it is living out the recognition of just how common we are —as common as bread. Humility, as Thomas Merton reminds us, is about coming to the understanding that we are not the exception, good or bad. We are linked with all of creation through the most basic and unarguable thread: our existence. No one chooses to be born, to hatch, to sprout; not an okra seed, not a baby finch, not a child. All of creation exists by no volition of its own, and that is perhaps the greatest insult to the human illusion of control there ever was. No wonder we spend our lifetimes trying to prove our worth or value, trying to earn or run from what we think we deserve.

For me, grace is a patchwork quilt Christ wraps around me each and every time I notice the nakedness of my condition. He does this not to hide my nakedness for his sake—after all, the link between nakedness and shame is a human invention—but out of mercy and love for me. So I will stop being enamored or consumed with my own nakedness, my embarrassments, failures, plans, and image.

When I am clothed in the patchwork covering of grace, my focus is taken off myself and I am able to look away from my own condition, fully aware of it but no longer consumed by it, and back into the face of Christ—opening my eyes, my heart, and my ears to Christ's call on my life, the call to live out grace through humility and service, loving others with the same wild abandon Christ has for me.

"See that scrap there?" he says pointing to one particularly frayed edge of the quilt. "That is my most beloved child. Go bake him a pie. And see this patch over here?" he says, pointing to a rather large and garish piece of fabric. "This is my beloved child. I know she is loud and awkward, but I love her. Now go talk to her, be her friend."

But of course, even wrapped in the loveliest of all quilts, I, like the disciples before me, want to remain comfortable. I balk. I complain. I whine.

"Yes, you are naked," Christ says to me. "You have made mistakes. You weren't prepared. You have been shown up. Your plan stank. You are imperfect. You are no better or worse than anyone else. This is not news to me. I love you. Can we move on now? I need you to make dinner."

And so, again and again, I gather the flour, the butter, the water, and the leftover chicken and begin to find a way to use whatever I have, wherever I am, to say, "Yes, Lord," with each push of the rolling pin.

Patchwork Pot Pie Recipe

Ingredients for the filling

1 cup frozen vegetable mix (green beans, corn, carrots)

1 cup frozen broccoli

1 can of white meat chicken, drained

Leftover rotisserie chicken meat, chopped up (about 1½ cups)

1 large leftover baked potato or 2 medium boiled potatoes, cut into slices

½ yellow onion, chopped

Salt and pepper to taste

3 tablespoons of flour

1 cup chicken broth

Ingredients for the crust

2½ cups all-purpose flour

1 teaspoon salt

2 sticks chilled salted butter, cut into 1-inch cubes

Cold ice water

Directions

- Preheat oven to 375 degrees Fahrenheit.
- Begin by making the crust. First, mix the 2½ cups of all-purpose flour with the salt, then cut in the chilled salted butter cubes. (I use my food processor, though a pastry cutter works just fine.) Once the mixture is all crumbly, start adding ice cold water, one tablespoon at a time, pulsing the food processor between each tablespoon until the crumbly mixture becomes a solid ball of dough. Wrap the dough in plastic wrap and place it in the freezer to rest.
- Prepare the meat and vegetable filling ingredients. Toss together in a large bowl and sprinkle with 3 tablespoons of flour.
- Remove dough from freezer and cut in half.
- Roll each half out on a floured surface into an approximately 9-inch circle.

- Remove one circle from the floured surface and place in the pie pan. If the circle falls apart or splits into pieces, no worries. This is where the patchwork part comes in. Simply begin adding the pieces to your pie pan, pressing and patching each bit together until the entire bottom and inside rim of the dish is covered.
- Pour veggie-meat mixture into the piecrust.
- Add chicken broth. Sprinkle flour over the mixture.
- Cover the pie with the second circle of dough. Again, if the dough breaks while you are transferring, just patchwork it together.
- Bake for 30-40 minutes or until the middle of the pie is bubbly and the crust is golden.
- Allow the pie to cool and set for 15-20 minutes before serving.

chapter 16

Hospitality, Soup Kitchens, and Lenten Dinners

Love people. Cook them tasty food.
—Bumper Sticker from Penzey's Spice Store

Special attention should be given to the needy guest.
Material wants should be attended to in a way that
preserves dignity.
—John McQuiston II

Every family has a talent. Something they can offer the world. The Von Trapp family had music, the Baldwins, acting, and the Mannings, football. Our family's talent is food, cooking, and serving.

Arkansas is one of those states where everyone talks about the weather, the running joke being: "If you don't like the weather, just wait five minutes. It will change." In the central part of the state where we live, it is common to get some small dustings of snow in January and February, and every few years there is a major ice storm or two. But just as snow and ice are possible in February, so is a week of eighty-five-degree highs. I stopped packing my winter and summer clothes away in boxes long ago, there being little point in it. Instead I shuffle my thinnest and thickest clothes from the playroom closet to my own closet as needed. This past December the weather was so warm I wore open-toed sandals to see a revival of *Home Alone* at the movie theater; I painted my toenails red and green to help me get in the holiday spirit. I spent Christmas Day on the deck chair soaking up the sun. Of course, by New Year's Day we had the fireplace roaring and my festive toes were hidden in furry boots. In between, our pond flooded during a torrential downpour. So you can see why weather is a part of the conversation around here.

Personally, I love snow days, hate ice storms, and growl when temperatures go above forty-five in the winter. But as lovely as the snow is, and as inconvenient as the ice is with our cars and houses and heating bills, winter weather is brutal— and occasionally lethal—for our homeless neighbors. When Wylie was a baby and ice took out the power at my parents' on Christmas Day, at least we had shelter, dry blankets, a gas stove to cook food on, and working indoor plumbing. That Christmas was the coldest we have ever spent, but my memory of it is filled with the comfort and joy we found in being all together, huddled around a stove, making kettle after kettle of French press coffee.

For our homeless neighbors, that frozen Christmas was a vastly different experience. A snow forecast used to send me into a happy dance in anticipation of a warm and cozy day spent at home, baking and making, the whole world outside covered in a blanket of sparkly white. But then I met Aaron Reddin, and now I no longer rejoice so easily. Aaron runs a nonprofit called The One, Inc., with the mission to meet the needs of our homeless neighbors. He and his friends helped our family understand that what we find beautiful and tranquil about a snow day includes things that can be deadly to our homeless neighbors. Which is why, over the past few years, Aaron and other community organizers have worked hard each winter to create a system of "warming shelters" in local churches and schools in areas where there are dense homeless populations. Our homeless friends and citizens can get out of the weather for the night and receive a hot meal or two. Four years ago, we experienced one of those harsh, icy, brutally cold winters. It seemed as if Aaron and his friend Dennis would never have enough volunteers to provide meals and shelter for everyone affected by the storms. But they persevered and rallied every church and organization they could.

Aaron, more than anyone, has dramatically changed the way I think about Christian hospitality. He refers to the homeless people in our community as friends and neighbors—mostly his friends. Also, he abhors the term "feeding the homeless" because, as he says, "You feed animals at the zoo; you share meals with your friends." And he should know, because Aaron was homeless himself once, and experienced firsthand all the ways do-gooder Christians—intentionally or not—put up safe walls between themselves and those whom they serve. When Aaron sent out the call for shelter and sustenance for his friends, the little church we were then a part of was one of the many (but not enough, never enough) faith communities who answered the call to provide a dinner for a hundred or so of our coldest neighbors.

R Street Community Church has never been a big church, but the heart of this small community was—and is to this day—huge. And for all the things R Street doesn't have—a lot of programs, a fancy building, a large congregation—the one thing it has in abundance is a passion to serve, to be the hands and feet of Christ on the earth, to be Jesus with skin on in the community. As the winter weather began to move into Central Arkansas that year, it was obvious there would never be an opportunity better than this one to live out that passion.

In a previous life, as I've mentioned, Nathan was a banquet chef, so the task of planning the meal fell to him. He decided on a huge pot of kitchen sink soup, a vat of slaw, and warm bread. While a crew of R Street adults and teens worked in the tiny, cramped kitchen at the back of the storefront church serving as the warming center, the rest of us set out cookies and baked goods we had brought, and helped set up table and chairs. Whole families had shown up to serve Aaron and his friends.

When the meal took a little longer to cook than expected, and the line grew restless, the kids gathered up baskets of muffins and took them down the row, offering one to each man and woman. I will never forget the sight of four-year-old Violet and six-year-old Miles offering muffins to some of the roughest, dirtiest people I have ever met. They would hold up their baskets, look each person in the eye, and ask, "Would you like a muffin while you wait?" Miles earned the moniker Muffin Man that night, and his memories are of a "really fun night."

Some of the teenagers and adults not working in the kitchen played cards with those waiting to eat, while others, like my friend Kitzel, ministered to those who appeared to be in pain, or who needed someone to listen to their story. Once the meal line was flowing steadily, Nathan, along with Mark and the rest of their band, played while the kids, their baskets full of homemade cookies this time, visited the overflowing tables and couches and chairs. The rest of us sat down with our neighbors to also enjoy bowls of soup and cornbread.

Later, as Nathan was cleaning up the last of the pots and pans, Aaron told him how much the night meant to him. To have a home-cooked, healthy meal filled to overflowing with wholesome ingredients and vegetables is a rare gift in the warming shelters. Many churches send pizzas or boxes of fried chicken—well-intentioned but lacking in the nutrition that those who live on the streets and in the camps out in the woods so desperately need. All too often, there is an attitude that the have-nots should be satisfied with the leftovers and castoffs of the haves, and this extends to food as well as clothes and furnishings. Again, I have to think about what it means to serve "the least." *Whenever you did one of these things to someone overlooked or ignored, that was me—you did it to me*, Jesus says in the Gospel according to Matthew (25:40 MSG). As a confessed hostessing addict, I am fairly confident that if Jesus were coming over for dinner, I wouldn't pick up a bucket of chicken or a five-dollar one-topping pizza. I would pull out all the stops. Not because Jesus would expect the best, or be offended by pizza, but because spoiling people with amazing food is how I love my family, my friends, and hopefully the stranger.

Sara Miles, in *Take This Bread: A Radical Conversation* (a must-read, by the way), writes, "There's a hunger beyond food that's expressed in food, and that's why feeding is always a kind of miracle." This is the miracle we saw that night at the warming center. To see clean and happy middle-class children interacting fearlessly with their homeless neighbors, to watch those neighbors' eyes light up at the sight of fresh vegetables, and to see a crusty and weather-beaten face crack a toothless smile while playing cards with the clean-cut teenage boy who sees not a stranger but a friend—these are gifts that helped make that night memorable for so many of us. I am not sure the gifts we gave changed any of our neighbors' lives, or that any of them remember the Muffin Man or the music Mark and Nathan shared. But these experiences changed the way a lot of us will interact with and think about the homeless in our communities. We went into the night doing our best to be Jesus for our neighbors, and in the end we realized how much more they were being Jesus to us. They are the ignored and overlooked, and if I am to believe Jesus, then those crusty, toothless, awkward, and smelly people to whom Miles offered muffins—they are Jesus.

Years after the warming shelter meal, our family took on another feed-a-crowd challenge. We offered to cook, serve, and clean up all our church's Lenten dinners. By tradition, these dinners are served one weeknight each of the six weeks of Lent in conjunction with a Bible or book study, and are typically simple suppers, almost austere, in keeping with the trademark bareness of the Lenten season. But as new Episcopalians, we were not yet privy to all of the ways our church observed the bareness and desertlike conditions of the season. All we knew was this: dinner was needed, Lent was early, and the weather was atrociously bitter. Winter is hard, dark, and cold enough without our help. And as I've said, our family loves people by filling them up with hearty food. Blissfully unaware, we set ourselves the goal of making sure each church member, each week, left warm and full. We cooked lasagna and spaghetti and roast chicken and savory bread pudding. We served French dip sandwiches and hearty beef soup and chicken enchilada casserole. We made huge salads and homemade dressings. But, because it was Lent, we never served dessert. I did have the good sense to know that much.

When we offered to make the meals, we were aware of the sacrifice we would make. We could have bought large premade frozen meals at Sam's Club, or gone the canned soup and soda cracker route. But we chose to cook the meals ourselves for three reasons: we wanted to honor the dignity of our fellow church members by taking the time to cook them homemade dinners; we wanted to be inconvenienced by the experience (as part of our Lenten discipline); and we wanted to involve our kids in the process as much as possible. We sought to interrupt our comfort—and the comfort of our kids—for the sake of our community, digging into the vow of Stability we had made, doing our best to live out the command of Jeremiah 29 to work for the welfare of our community.

Our first step was to plan each meal by making a menu and shopping list on the Friday or Saturday preceding the meal. Sunday afternoons were for grocery shopping, hitting the bulk food and grocery stores. My job on Sunday nights was to make the family dinner so Nathan could focus on prepping the church meal—dicing vegetables, reducing stock, caramelizing onions. We ate a lot of meals those six weeks consisting of a rotisserie chicken or casserole from the deli section, with a baguette and a salad. On Monday nights, it was more of the same—Nathan handling the next level of Lenten supper prep and me taking care of our dinner: premarinated pork tenderloins, steam-bag veggies, microwaved sweet potatoes. I chose things I could make without hogging the stovetop or what little counter space we had. While our dinner cooked, the boys and I did what we could to help—slicing cherry tomatoes for the salads, buttering the sliced Italian loaves, grating cheese to top the casseroles. Once we had prepped as much as we could, our next step was to pack everything in reusable tubs and dishes to transport it to the church immediately after work and school on Tuesday.

Tuesdays, we would work fast to get everything ready. Nathan heated or baked whatever still needed to be cooked. The boys set the tables with burlap runners and votive candles, salt and pepper shakers, and baskets of bread or chips. Typically, I put together the salad, set out the serving trays, and helped direct the boys. Our friends Josh and Katie made huge vats of tea, lemonade, and ice water. We set out all the plates, flatware, and napkins, and waited for the prayer service to conclude and the doors to open wide, ushering in cold and hungry parishioners. Each of us took a place behind the counter and served up the meal, heaping spoonfuls of casserole and salad onto each plate.

After the meal, we closed the serving window between the kitchen and dining area and begin to clean while the rest of the group moved into the book study. The boys gathered and scraped plates and washed pans. Nathan ran cycle after cycle of the industrial dishwasher, and I dried and put away dishes. When there were leftovers, we bagged up one-meal portions and set them out on the counter for folks to take home for the next day's lunch or dinner. We wanted none of the food to be wasted, and everyone's bellies to be filled. Finally, at the very end, Wylie and Miles would go back out and quietly gather the table runners and candles, putting them away in the closet until the next week.

Months later I would realize just how out-of-the-box and extravagant those "simple suppers" had been, and I would laugh in embarrassment at my mistake. But in all honesty, I will never regret one single dish we served. Many of the people who came to our Lenten suppers lived on very limited, fixed incomes, and seeing their excitement as we revealed each week's menu was worth breaking any informal liturgical "rule" of the season.

Barbara Brown Taylor once said, "Our lives are inextricably bound up with the lives of other people," and that, like it or not, is completely true. We are not islands, despite our best efforts at times to live that way. My family's talent is cooking and serving food, so it makes sense for us to use this talent when serving the welfare of our community. By continuing to look for and participate in opportunities for our family to use this talent, we are teaching our children that they have a responsibility to all with whom their lives are bound: the neighbor, the church member, the mailperson, the salesclerk, the teacher, the bus driver, the kid who smells funny. We are all bound up in each other's lives, but we have a choice in how we live in this state. Do we love? And if so, what does loving look like? And this is God's plan for humanity: to be inextricably connected to each other and to learn to care for and love each other here on earth. Simply, to give and to receive.

For almost our entire married life, my husband and I have had the luxury of extended family living nearby or even with us. For years, my in-laws lived ten minutes away, and all of my siblings have at some point over the past two decades lived in our guest room or on our couch. When Wylie was a baby, my sister-in-law lived in an apartment in our neighborhood. But recently, there was a time when no one lived near us. My in-laws had moved to Louisiana, and my siblings were spread from Texas to Montana. In this window of family abandonment (how dare they have lives of their own!), Nathan and I both got the flu. The everything-aches-fevers-chills-elephant-on-your-head flu, both of us so sick that we could not drive or cook or handle things like getting the boys to school. And even though (thankfully) both our boys were old enough to get themselves dressed, make a box of mac-n-cheese, and put themselves to bed at a decent hour, there was still one major hurdle: neither of them could drive a car.

No way to get groceries, or medicine (which we were completely out of), or any way to get the boys to school. We had found ourselves in our late thirties, alone and bereft, for the first time without biological family to do these things for us. We needed help. It was time for drastic measures, and I only did what any self-respecting mother of the digital age would do: I updated my Facebook status. I posted a half-dead, sufficiently pitiful update about our condition, and when our friends and acquaintances began to ask if they could help, I humbly said, for the first time ever, "Yes, please."

I said yes to Ann's offer to go to the grocery store for us, yes to Sarah's offer to help get the boys to school and back, and yes, please yes, to Heather's offer to make us homemade chicken noodle soup. We drank the juice Ann bought us and we ate a dozen bowls of the amazing, healing soup Heather made for us. We gratefully sent the boys to school in Sarah's care each morning and we watched through our blurry, feverish eyes as our boys grew up another rung that week—caring for each other while Nathan and I lay in our sickbed, powerless even to make them PB&J sandwiches.

A dictionary definition of the word *hospitality* is "the friendly and generous reception and entertainment of guests, visitors, or strangers." When Nathan and I had the flu, we became the guests, and all of those friends the hostesses, bringing their generous reception to our doorstep. Rumi said, "This being human is a guesthouse," which makes me think of all the ways we are receiving and hosting others, and being received and hosted daily. We are guesthouses. All of us. And if we want to live as Christ, we must generously receive all who come to us—whether it is to serve or be served. We must open up the doors of our being, of our guesthouse, and we must have the humility to be both host and guest, in all that we say and do.

We live in a culture obsessed with food, but also of a split mind—we are foodies and bulimics at once. We want it all—we want to eat amazing food and we want none of it to show on our hips. Because of this, our relationship to sharing meals has grown ridiculously complicated. But nowhere in the Gospel does Jesus seem concerned with weight, food trends, fusion restaurants, or calorie trackers. He does seem concerned with hunger—the widows, the orphans, the birds, the outcast, and the forgotten. I am not the first, nor will I be the last, to find it interesting that one of the patterns we see in the Gospels is Jesus sharing meals with others. Picnics, formal dinners, impromptu gatherings—Jesus seems to be eating or talking about eating quite a bit. And he ate with everyone—strangers, family, crowds, best friends, prostitutes. He goes to weddings and funerals, he invites himself over for dinner, and he makes sure the multitudes get their fishes and loaves. Jesus is no stranger to hospitality—the giving or the receiving of it.

In Jeremiah 29 God tells his people to "work for the peace and prosperity of the city where I sent you into exile. Pray to the LORD for it, for its welfare will determine your welfare" (Jer. 29:7 NLT). St. Benedict says in his Rule, "All guests who arrive should be received as Christ. . . . One must adore Christ in them, for he is in fact the one who is received." If this is true, if Christ is in the least, the overlooked, the ignored, the dismissed, if we are to work and pray for our communities (even if they are hostile), then here is the unbridled truth of what I think: I think we should give it all away. Who cares if it is "deserved"? (I cannot figure out how to create that unit of measurement anyhow.)

If someone asks you for a dollar in the Target parking lot, give it to them.

Someone is rude to you in the carpool line? Smile.

Share meals with the hungry *and* the full.

Be a friend to the lonely *and* the popular. (We do not know what is behind the facade—whether someone is dressed in rags or designer jeans.)

What does it cost us to give these things away? Pride? Arrogance? Entitlement? Being "right"? Retribution? Things being fair?

Why do we hold so tightly to our stuff and our beliefs about how people should behave and live?

Over and over and over in the Gospels we see Jesus modeling for us how he wants us to live. At no time did he go into his house, lock the doors, and numb himself to the needs in the world. Instead, time and time again, we see Jesus saying to someone along the road, "Come along with me. Let's go eat."

So how can we as individuals and families begin to live out the liturgy of hospitality? How can we do the work of being a guesthouse for our fellow humans? I suggest we start by invoking the words of my favorite bumper sticker: *Love people. Cook them tasty food.*

Let us cook meals for our white middle-class church and for our homeless neighbors.

Let us cook meals for our best friends and for the interfaith gatherings in our community.

Let us cook meals for the homebound at Christmas and for the children at vacation Bible school.

Let us cook meals for the teachers. For the students. For the parents.

Let us cook meals for our book club and for the sick and the dying.

Let us cook meals for the new parents and for the couple getting divorced.

Let us cook meals for each other and for the stranger.

And may we adore Christ within each person we meet and may we cook them tasty food.

chapter 17

Widows, Orphans, Deep Gladness, and Nest Fluffing

The homes I like the best are totally occupied, busy, and useful, whether it's a tiny little house or a great big one. Rarely do you find a great big house that's used in a good way. So I prefer smaller spaces that are full of books, full of things that people are doing.
—Martha Stewart

The guest quarters should be entrusted to a God-fearing brother. Adequate bedding should be available there. The house of God should be in the care of wise men who will manage it wisely.
—The Rule of St. Benedict

I have found that quite often I get exactly what I ask for, but rarely how I imagined it.

Once upon a time, in an economy far, far away, interior design work was my bread and butter. In between the ministry years, and before the writing began in earnest, I was employed to decorate people's homes. I would design their window treatments, oversee their remodels, and on occasion paint their furniture. I shopped for throw pillows, bossed contractors around, and kept a box of paint chips in my car. While I was never the fanciest, or the best, or the trendiest designer in town, I did try to be the most personal. No matter how large or small the job, I would always do my best to learn as much about the client as possible—their story, their history, their hobbies, their great loves, their dreams, their family—before I developed a design plan for their home. Always a storyteller at heart, I saw my job as an opportunity to help my clients tell their story, or rewrite their story if needed. Sometimes this storytelling was part of a healing process: decorating a new home after a divorce; settling into a smaller house after a foreclosure; turning what should have been a nursery into an art studio. So I would look for old typewriters for the writer and commission sketches of pets for the animal lover and scrounge through attics for old land maps for the landowner. During those years, I found a great gladness in creating homes that told the stories of those who lived there, and I found great joy in creating spaces that provided warmth, comfort, and happiness for all who entered.

But while I loved bringing meaning to the design process, I also wrestled with the true value in what I was doing. Surely decorating houses isn't as worthy as saving orphans in Africa or rescuing women out of the sex traffic trade. I seriously doubted picking out lamps and having couches recovered, no matter how much intention I gave those choices, could do as much to advance the kingdom of God here on earth as going out to homeless camps in the middle of ice storms to make sure the people were safe.

As a good Baptist preacher's kid, I knew what service for God looked like—I knew true dedication to God's leading meant hardship, sacrifice, and dying to self over and over. As a child I had seen pictures of the missionary families our church supported all over the world and cringed at the obvious self-sacrifice those families were making for the sake of Christ. I mean, one look at their out-of-date clothes and hairstyles and their selflessness was obvious. For years, I would pray that God would not call me to the mission field, so I wouldn't have to wear ugly clothes. (Only years later, as a college student, I met a whole group of former missionary kids who were as fashionable as anyone else, and learned that most of those pictures I'd seen were taken during the first year of a family's service, sometimes twenty years earlier.)

But still this idea remained: sacrifice and selflessness and the question of meaning and self-denial. In the back of my mind was always this question: Is what I do really worthy? In those years when I bought lampshades and had couches recovered, I did so always hoping that I was helping create warm, safe, inviting, comforting, inspiring places for the people who lived there. And yet there was always this nagging question: is my work frivolous?

During this season I heard a story on NPR about the Green House Project, a nursing home designed from the ground up to look and feel like a real home, the objective being that through this small home setup, professional caregivers can "return control, dignity, and a sense of well-being to elders." Driving down the freeway, I listened to the doctors, architects, and designers talk about how they had worked together to create an intentional, warm, nurturing, homelike environment for seniors whom many had given up on. Big roly-poly tears began to plop onto my steering wheel when they told of the patient who had not spoken for a year, until she was moved into a Green House home. Those doctors believed what I had long suspected: our physical environment matters, and it can be used to bring about healing to our bodies and our souls. And what they did seemed to fit the picture in my mind of what significant work looked like. They were helping to restore purpose to lives, and they were doing it through the physical environment right where their patients lived.

Maybe this was a way I, too, could provide meaning in my work. Listening to the show, I made a promise to myself that if an opportunity like the Green House Project ever came my way, I would fight tooth and nail to be a part of it.

A year or two later, when the bottom fell out of the housing market, the economy tanked, and the demand for middle-class decorators dried up, I left the interior design world and found a more predictable paycheck courtesy of our local library and our boys' school. Even though I had left the designing life professionally, my love of "fluffing my nest," as my Paw used to say, remained.

In the months we waited for our house to sell so we could move to the farm, I began to gather ideas for the little shack of a house. Convinced I could work a miracle on the interior, I started secret Pinterest boards and begin pinning ideas for flooring, cabinetry, wall treatments, light fixtures, and paint colors. I even went as far as creating mood boards for several of the rooms and posted them on my blog. I would lie in bed awake, staring at the ceiling, mentally going through every stick of furniture we owned, trying to decide what we would sell, give away, and take with us.

Of course, the story is now well-known. We never bought that house. The sale on our house fell through, our offer on the farm expired, and everything went pear-shaped, the last straw being when I broke my foot in three places right before the autumn and winter holidays. Which is how, sitting on my couch for three months, my foot propped up, unable to walk or drive or run, I discovered the verses of Jeremiah 29:4–14, verses written to people who were living in exile, far from the home they longed for. Also, I stumbled upon a little thing called the Rule of St. Benedict, a set of teachings to help Benedictine monks live lives as unto God with grateful hearts, in whatever situation they found themselves, in whatever location, with whatever group of people. And these writings—the verses in Jeremiah, the teachings of St. Benedict—through the work of the Holy Spirit, had begun to reshape my heart. In the months after my foot healed, as I began to walk again, I also began to try and live out the instructions given by God through Jeremiah and by St. Benedict: instructions such as *Build houses and make yourself at home* (Jer. 29:4), and *Pursue the peace and welfare of your city* (7), and *Great care and concern are to be shown in receiving poor people and pilgrims,* from chapter 53 of St. Benedict's Rule.

I wasn't really sure how I was going to build a house, considering the house I had wanted to rebuild had been sold to someone else, but I was willing to keep my options open. At the same time, I began to look for ways that we, as a family, could pursue the peace and welfare of our city, and how we could begin showing better care and concern for the poor and the pilgrims all around us. One night, scanning through Facebook, ignoring the dishes and the laundry, I saw that my friend Aaron, who runs the local nonprofit that serves our homeless neighbors, The One, Inc., was raising money to buy a house for an emergency refuge for homeless women and children. This refuge would be red-tape-free, allowing women and their children in without the hoops required by other local shelters. Frederick Buechner famously wrote, "The place God calls you to is the place where your deep gladness and the world's deep hunger meet." As soon as I read Aaron's post I knew that this was a place where my deep gladness in creating warm, comforting, personal spaces could meet a real and tangible need. So without hesitation, I sent Aaron a flurry of text messages that went something like this:

> *Hey. I want to coordinate the decorating and furnishing of this house.*
> *And I want to do it right. No college dorm hand-me-downs.*
> *I want it to be nicer than my house. I want it to be comfortable and nurturing. I believe spaces can heal and give hope and that's what I want this house to be.*

And no one would put Jesus on a ratty sofa, why would we put a homeless
mother on one?

Okay I don't mean to flood your inbox. You can tell me no.

Please let me do this.

Once Aaron recovered from the onslaught of my rapid-fire texts, he responded with a huge and happy YES. The One, Inc., had grown exponentially in its short few years. He had a lot to juggle and spending hours picking out curtains and sofas was clearly not the best use of his time. But it was a great use of mine. As soon as the papers were signed on the house, Aaron gave me the green light, and my nest-fluffing skills went into overdrive.

Going forward I knew two things: I wanted to be intentional about every piece of furniture and every decoration that went into the house; and I wanted to honor the Benedictine practice of hospitality, giving "special attention to the needy . . . attending to material wants in a way that gives dignity." I wanted to furnish and fluff this house as unto the least of those in our community.

I believe that things like wall color, fabric choice, wall art, and lighting matter. Not in a "we must have the best" or "we must have the trendiest" sort of way, but in the way my grandmother's house makes me feel as if anything is possible every single time I visit. Or the way Pottery Barn always smells clean and safe. Or the way Anthropologie inspires me to get all funky-crafty, my creative juices swirling at warp speed within minutes of walking through the door. Or how I feel when I kneel at the altar rail at our church and remember to notice the stained-glass windows to my left (Creation) and to my right (the new Jerusalem), reminding me that I am right where I was created to be—in the middle of God's story, living in community. Each of these spaces evokes a specific feeling and tells a specific story, and all of it is well thought out. Pottery Barn has spent a lot of time and money learning how to make us believe that with the right deep-seated couch, plush rug, and warm lighting, our home will feel like a refuge, our marriage will last, our children will pick up their toys, and nothing will ever smell bad.

It doesn't take long, reading the Rule, to realize that St. Benedict was a big fan of intentional living. I dare say he was also a fan of going slow and digging in. Why else would he interrupt perfectly productive days to pray? While St. Benedict doesn't say much about the physical space of an abbey, his few statements on the subject reverberate with the need for a deliberate and thoughtful approach to setting up house.

> *The surroundings of the monastery should, if possible, be so constructed that within it all necessities, such as water, mill and garden are contained, and the various crafts are practiced. Then there will be no need for the monks to roam outside, because this is not at all good for their souls.*

Wanting to love the women and children who would seek refuge at The One house as soon as possible, getting them off the streets and into warm beds, the first call I made after Aaron gave me the green light was to our friends Mark and Keith, asking if they would build the initial three sets of bunk beds through their group, the Bed Project. The Bed Project had begun some years earlier in Mark's garage, with a handful of teenagers and adults who wanted to build beds for families in need.

Someone once asked why they don't simply use the money for the wood (which is not cheap) to buy inexpensive metal bunk beds for these families (which would be faster), and I love Mark's reply so much, that instead of trying to summarize it, I'll let him tell you:

This has been a persistent question, and we have discussed this among ourselves at length over the years. Those discussions were never simple. In most cases, we were intentional about building a particular type of bed. The reasons to build rather than purchase a simple bed frame were varied, and, when taken together, were compelling to us.

Providing beds to those in need was not our sole aim; we also had a spiritual formation aim, specifically to develop compassion. The project tried to balance these aims. What was efficient for one aim was not necessarily efficient for the other. We felt that the process of building our own beds forced us to face the means of and obstacles to compassion. We structured the project in a way that put us together over time and in a variety of activities. The contemporary means and obstacles we faced provided rich material for us to process through ongoing discussion and contemplation, which we felt was good for spiritual formation.

We also wanted to learn to love well. Building the beds allowed us to give a piece of ourselves with the beds. Beyond utility, we hoped our beds conveyed dignity to those receiving them. For us, this meant building with attention to detail and beauty, and a bed of no less quality than we would want for ourselves. We considered this an expression of love and value of the recipients.

Develop compassion, love well, convey dignity. These are the exact things The One, Inc., is about, and why the Bed Project was such a great fit for this project.

I believe the love that the Bed Project guys put into building the beds stays with those beds. That their energy of compassion, humility, and dignity soaked into the wood frames, and remains with those beds to this day, comforting each and every person who sleeps there. If Einstein was right, if E really does equal MC squared, if everything is really made up of energy, then who is to say this isn't possible? This is why we bless things in the church, isn't it? So the energy of our love and prayers is connected to the energy and love of God, and poured into and over the very thing we have blessed. This is how it is with every pillowcase and every measuring cup that came into the house—each item came with the love and blessings of those who sent it.

Once we had the beds, there were mattresses, blankets, sheets, and pillows to bring in. And that was just the bedrooms. This was a whole house we were furnishing. When I decorated Kathryn's House (as The One, Inc., house was officially named in honor of an unarmed homeless woman named Kathryn who was shot in the back in November 2014), I wanted to practice this same thoughtfulness with each item I purchased or requested. I made an inspiration board for each room of the house, picking out images of furniture and accessories I thought would work well with the house's architectural style and existing paint colors. From blankets to dishes to shower curtains, everything is chosen for its practicality, beauty, and most of all, its warm and comforting nature. The paintings and artwork impart messages of grace, courage, hope, redemption, and unconditional love. I wanted to create a space that would honor the dignity of each woman and child who entered, so I did my best to be thoughtful and deliberate in choosing decorative items that also conveyed the spiritual truth that they are loved and valued. I began with a hand-lettered sign my friend Tiffani created based on a prayer for her daughter Grace and generously donated to the house. Grace's Prayer seemed to sum up what everyone involved with Kathryn's House wanted for our homeless sisters and their children:

My heart for her is that she will learn that her journey is where she will become strong. Her strength is from God not within herself. She stands when no one else does. She speaks for those who cannot. That she be the light when everything else is dark. She has the eyes to see the lovely and the unlovely for that is so often where we see God. That she lives loved . . . because she knows she is loved by God. She hears his song over her each and every day . . . and that she's able to forgive because she knows the depths of her forgiveness.

And gifts like these were just the beginning. Knowing there are lots of people like me who love to shop but have more stuff than they can ever need, I thought: *What if people could shop for the house the same way you shop for a wedding or a baby shower—with a registry? Would they help? Couldn't hurt to try!* With input from Aaron and his team, I made an online wish list at Target, choosing items that were warm and cheerful in tone and texture, registering for everything from measuring spoons to bedding to coffee mugs to desks. Once the list was finished, we posted the link on my blog and The One, Inc.'s Facebook page urging people to turn their love of shopping into a redemptive act. *Why not shop for a cause?* I posted. *Dying to order that adorable new poof ottoman from Target? Do it! But send it to us!* I urged my readers. Before we knew it packages began arriving from all over the country. Kid President even sent out the call for donations on our behalf. We received curtains from New York, pillows from California, dishes from Texas.

And the fun didn't stop there. A local cabinetmaker built banquette seating in the awkwardly long breakfast nook. Friends offered to wash the sheets and make the beds and pick up donations from around town. Washers, dryers, sofas, mattresses, televisions, entertainment centers, rocking chairs, Pack 'n Plays, and toys for the kids were all donated by individuals and companies. The pantry was stocked and toiletry kits filled the bathroom cabinets, thanks to the work of local youth groups. And artists from around the country donated beautiful original paintings and prints, all with happy, encouraging, life-giving images and words. Words that speak blessings and wholeness over all who enter.

Once most of the items were collected, our family spent several Saturdays at the house fluffing every nook and cranny. The boys unpacked box after box, helped make beds, and washed all the new cookware and utensils. Nathan hung curtain rods and put together the entertainment centers and helped me move beds. It took three times as long as we had anticipated—due to life, plus burst pipes and plumbing issues—but finally the house was ready. Together, as a huge community, one stretching as far as our country's borders (in large part thanks to Kid President's help), we had created a warm, clean, inviting, and safe home for homeless women and children to find refuge.

I happily passed the fluffing baton on to Kara, the house manager, who now is doing the real work—the grace-filled, hard, exhausting, amazing work of loving the women and children who come through the doors of Kathryn's House. It is Kara and other volunteers who—to this day—continue to make the house a home for all who enter, opening the doors wide, making sure the beds are made and the food warm.

When I began the process of looking for a way to use my great gladness to meet a need in my community, I had no idea where it would lead. At the time I was mourning the loss of a dream home—a house I thought I wanted and a life I was sure would make me happier. Instead I had the chance, my family had the chance, to help birth a home that gives shelter to widows and orphans, the poor and the lonely. By using my great gladness, my seemingly silly, frivolous gladness of picking out lampshades and window treatments, I had the opportunity to help bring peace to our city. A home that is safe and dry, a home that helps satisfy the hunger for home and belonging so many women and children in our community face.

When we are able to pair our great gladness with the world's great need, we are able to enter into the story of redemption instead of just observing it. When we can bring our expertise, our knowledge, and our talents to those who are hungry for them, a beautiful alchemy takes place and a new relationship is birthed, a bond is created, an understanding formed. These intersections of gladness and need don't always present themselves to us on a platter; they aren't always as obvious as Kathryn's House was to me. Sometimes we must dig deeper, look behind corners and assumptions that are scary and challenging. But if we keep our eyes open, if we take some initiative to seek them out, we will always find them.

The day we made the last bed and hung the last picture, I realized I had indeed built a house. It wasn't the house I had planned on building, but it was a house all the same. And even better, it was a home. A home for widows and orphans, the poor and the pilgrim, the lonely and the lost. A home to help families thrive, a home to comfort and encourage. And while it might not have a barn or twenty acres, this home does have open doors, comfortable, sturdy beds with soft, clean sheets, and grace and love to spare, right in the middle of all the beauty and all the mess.

How to Throw a Free Garage Sale Fundraiser

If you are like me, you might like to shop, maybe a little too much. And maybe some of your friends like to shop. And maybe you have too much stuff. And your kids have too much stuff, and your spouse has too much stuff. Even your hamster is drowning in stuff. So, what good can come from all this stuff? Well, if you take notes from my friend Sarabeth, a lot of good can come from it. Sarabeth and her friends have been throwing Free Garage Sales for a couple of years now. They have raised crazy amounts of money for local charities and good works with these things. Begin in your home by looking around. What do you have that means little or nothing to you? Be intentional about your culling. Here's Sarabeth's advice:

Hosting a Giveaway Garage Sale, by Sarabeth Jones

Let me be clear about a couple of things right off the bat. First, I think this is the best fundraising idea ever. It's brilliant. Second, it is totally not my idea. I first heard about it from an e-mail newsletter that I subscribed to about decluttering your home, from a woman who called herself Flylady. She shared it as a wonderful way to rid yourself of unused stuff. We decided to try it and give the money to charity. It worked fabulously.

Here's what you do: have a garage sale where you give everything away. For free. No pricing, no haggling, just throw your stuff out on tables in your yard and give it away. Set up a bucket for donations and a sign telling where the money will go. We've done this several times now and had a great time, raised lots of money, and got rid of stuff we didn't need. Win, win, win!

Here are my tips for having a great giveaway:

1. **Invite others in. People love to help a good cause, and there are lots of ways to help with this.** I usually post the sale information on social media and ask people to drop off stuff at my house to give away, or volunteer to help set up or staff the

sale, or come shop and donate on sale day. People have donated washers and dryers, furniture, TVs, artwork, even an elliptical machine!

2. Make it a party. Make homemade cinnamon rolls and hot coffee to give away in cold weather, or cookies and lemonade if it's hot. Offer it to people (for free!) as they walk up. They are so surprised and happy that they'll already want to leave a donation, even if it's small. Play music. Dress up in the donated wedding dress. Have fun!

3. Inform people about your cause. I always have someone at the sale who understands and deeply cares about the cause we are supporting so that they can tell people a little about it as they are donating. You never know who is going to want to know more, or who is already connected in some way, or who might give a little more. It's amazing to see.

4. Be ruthless with your stuff. This is a great opportunity to do more than one good thing at a time, so take full advantage. Get the stuff out of your house; give the money to something good!

5. Let go of your expectations. It is not helpful to think about how much an item might bring at a "real" garage sale. If you want to have a sale with pricing and haggling and headaches—then have at it! The beauty of this is that it puts everyone on the same side: helping someone who needs it. And it works in a bunch of ways— some people who show up at your sale are going to find things they need and can't afford. Some people who are going to take a washer and leave $3. Be happy for them! Others are going to pick up an old baseball hat and leave you $50 because they love what you are doing. Be happy for them as well.

Epilogue

Two years after I broke my foot, I wonderfully and unexpectedly stumbled into an amazing job opportunity, one that would require a move to a more rural community. So, we sold our house at long last, thanking her for all the gifts and lessons she had taught us over the years.

We bought a farm, and moved to The Next Thing at long last. I started a new job in a new town, my kids started a new school, and we found ourselves in a whole new world. And now, two years in, I can tell you this: we are having to learn to Be Here once again. We are learning how to be at home in our life all over, just in a new context. The kids are struggling with Can't We Go Back? And I fight the urge to scream, "I can't wait until Someday when fill-in-the-blank is done!" about *each* of the projects this fixer-upper on eight acres requires.

Here at the farm we are learning again to live a seamless liturgy at home—praying while we paint, practicing stewardship with a table saw, buying our pig feed from the local shop, opening our doors to new neighbors who think, vote, and believe very differently from us. I am doing my best to stay open to the Spirit's leading, and learning how to choose between what is good and what is best for our family in this season of our life. Nathan and I have had to continue to work on our marriage as a new move brought new challenges in listening and Mutual Obedience, and I am discovering all over the importance of inner and outer stillness, as I fight the urge to Do All the Things All at Once.

Building, Planting, Reaping, Raising, Connecting, Giving. These are the ways I have learned (and continue to learn) how to practice Stability, Conversion, and a long (slow) Obedience. These are the ways I root myself to the place and the people God has called me to, learning to be present to the life I have, one day at a time.

Notes

Introduction

xi   *That faith and love operate best*   Kathleen Norris, *Acedia and Me: A Marriage, Monks, and a Writer's Life* (New York: Riverhead Books, 2010), 191–192.

Chapter One: Mess

3   *If we pay attention to our tears*   Shauna Niequist, *Bread and Wine: A Love Letter to Life Around the Table with Recipes* (Grand Rapids, MI: Zondervan, 2013), 66.

5   *Phyllis's memoir*   Phyllis Tickle, *The Shaping of a Life: A Spiritual Landscape* (New York: Image Books, 2001).

6   *The prologue*   Phyllis Tickle, *What the Land Already Knows: Winter's Sacred Days (Stories from the Farm in Lucy)* (Chicago: Loyola Press, 2003), prologue xi.

Chapter Two: The Plan

11   *The great thing, if one can*   C. S. Lewis, *The Letters of C. S. Lewis to Arthur Greeves (1914-1963)*, ed. Walter Hooper (New York: Collier, 1986), 499.

Chapter Three: Running

13   *To put the world right in order*   Debra J. Snyder, PhD, *Intuitive Parenting: Listening to the Wisdom of Your Heart* (New York: Atria Paperback/Beyond Words, 2010), 156.

18   *Reading about the Rule in*   Dennis L. Okholm, *Monk Habits for Everyday People: Benedictine Spirituality for Protestants* (Grand Rapids, MI: Brazos Press, 2007).

18   *We want life to have meaning*   Kathleen Norris, *Acedia and me*, 190.

Chapter Five: Sitting

23   *You do not need to know*   Elena Malits, *The Solitary Explorer: Thomas Merton's Transforming Journey* (San Francisco: Harper & Row, 1980), 94.

Chapter Six: Stability, Stewardship, and Painting Walls

33   *To make old paint brushes pliable*   *Short-Cuts to Home Making* (Chicago: The American Family Magazine, 1952), 25.

36   *It is not perfection*   Joan Chittister, OSB, Norris, Kathleen (foreword). *Essential Monastic Wisdom: Writings on the Contemplative Life*, ed. Hugh Feiss (HarperSanFrancisco, 1999), 150.

38   *Benedict wants us to realize*   Joan Chittister, OSB, *Essential Monastic Wisdom*, 99.

39   *Portions of the book*   Mark Scandrette and Lisa Scandrette, *Free: Spending Your Time and Money on What Matters Most* (Downers Grove, IL: IVP, 2013).

41   *fourth stage of humility*   John McQuiston II, *Always We Begin Again: The Benedictine Way of Living, Revised Edition* (Harrisburg, PA: Morehouse Publishing, 2011), 41.

Chapter Seven: Simplicity, Fasting, and Laundry

44   *To whiten your linens*   *Short-Cuts to Home Making*, 42.

44   *Benedict is splendidly precise*   Esther De Waal, *A Life-Giving Way: A Commentary on the Rule of St. Benedict* (Collegeville, MN: Liturgical Press, 1995), 159.

48   *One of my favorite books*   Barbara Brown Taylor, *An Altar in the World: A Geography of Faith* (New York: HarperOne, 2009).

Chapter Eight: Stillness, Being, and Mending

58   *You've no idea . . .*   *Make and Mend for Victory* (New York: The Spool Cotton Company, 1942).

58   *When we are stricken*   Hermann Hesse, *Bäume: Betractungen Und Gedichte*, as quoted in Nalini Nadkarni, *Between Earth and Sky: Our Intimate Connections to Trees* (Berkeley, CA: University of California Press, 2009), 111.

63   *A center of stillness*   Dag Hammarskjöld, "Join Us," The Nobel Foundation, 1961, accessed January 18, 2017, http://www.nobelprize.org/nobel_prizes/peace/laureates/1961/hammarskjöld-acceptance.html.

65   *He who sits alone*   Benedicta Ward, trans., *The Desert Fathers: Sayings of the Early Christian Monks* (New York: Penguin, 2003), 8.

66   *I did then what I knew how to do*   Maya Angelou, as quoted by, Glennon Doyle Melton, *Carry On, Warrior: The Power of Embracing Your Messy, Beautiful Life* (New York: Scribner, 2014), 196.

Chapter Nine: Silence, Prayer, and Stitching

71   *Love is the voice*   e. e. cummings, *Selected Poems*, ed. Richard S. Kennedy (New York: Liverlight, 1994), 71.

71   *I myself am made*   Augusten Burroughs, *Magical Thinking: True Stories* (New York: Picador/St Martin's Press, 2005), 110.

74   *I don't want to sell anything*   *Say Anything.* Directed by Cameron Crowe. United States: Gracie Films/Twentieth Century Fox, 1989.

75   *soul speaks its truth*   Parker J. Palmer, *Let Your Life Speak: Listening for the Voice of Vocation* (San Francisco: Jossey-Bass, 1999), 7.

77   *There is no prayer*   Susan Conroy, *Mother Teresa's Lessons of Love and Secrets of Sanctity* (Huntington, IN: Our Sunday Visitor, 2003).

79   *Remember the value of silence*   John McQuiston II, *Always We Begin Again*, 35.

Chapter Ten: Sabbath

83   *There often comes a time*   Donald Ogden Stewart, *Perfect Behavior, A Guide for Ladies and Gentlemen in All Social Crises* (New York: George H. Doran, 1922), 138.

88   *It does seem to me*   Barbara Brown Taylor, "Divine subtraction,". *The Christian Century. Nov. 3, 1999.* Christiancentury.org/article/2011-07/divine-subtraction. Accessed March 27, 2017.

90   *The world exists*   Robert Farrar Capon, *The Supper of the Lamb: A Culinary Reflection* (Garden City, NY: Doubleday, 1969), 86.

92   *The golden rule*   Ken Shigematsu, *God in My Everything: How an Ancient Rhythm Helps Busy People Enjoy God* (Grand Rapids, MI: Zondervan, 2013), 42.

Chapter Eleven: Manual Labor, Restoration, and Thriving

96   *In a world*   Barbara Brown Taylor, *An Altar in the World*, Introduction xviii.

100   *I am changed*   Jonathan Wilson-Hartgrove, *Strangers at My Door: A True Story of Finding Jesus in Unexpected Guests* (New York: Convergent, 2013), 43.

102   *Healing is impossible*   Wendell Berry, *The Art of the Commonplace: The Agrarian Essays of Wendell Berry*, ed. Norman Wirzba (Washington, DC: Shoemaker & Hoard, 2003), 157.

103   *Redemption is physical*   Jana Riess, *Flunking Sainthood: A Year of Breaking the Sabbath, Forgetting to Pray, and Still Loving My Neighbor* (Brewster, MA: Paraclete Press, 2011), 31.

       Manual labor to my father   Mary Ellen Chase, *Always Look on the Bright Side: Celebrating Each Day to the Fullest*, ed. Alan Klein (Berkeley, CA: Viva Edition, 2013), 66.

104   *Complaining is the acid*   Joan Chittister, OSB, *Essential Monastic Wisdom*, 53.

Chapter Twelve: Mutual Support, Starting Seeds, Gardening

105   *A family is a place*   Gautama Buddha, *Collected Bodhi Leaves IV*: Numbers 91 to 121 (Kandy, Sri Lanka: Buddhist Publication Society, 2011), 96.

       Gardens are not made   Rudyard Kipling, "The Glory of the Garden," in Rudyard Kipling and C. R. L. Fletcher, *A History of England* (London: Henry Frowde and Hodder & Stoughton, 1911), 249.

109   *No one is excused*   John McQuiston II, *Always We Begin Again*, 53.

Chapter Thirteen: Conversion: Lessons from a Worm Farm

116   *There are more failures*   Roy E. Biles, *The Complete Book of Garden Magic* (Garden City, NY: Garden City Pub./Doubleday, 1947), 82.

Conversion is not the smooth   John Bunyan, quoted in *John Bunyan (1628–1688): His Life, Times and Work,* by John Brown (Boston: Houghton, Mifflin, 1888), 389.

120   *No one longs for what*   Barbara Brown Taylor, *An Altar in the World*, Introduction xvi-xvii.

121   *There is no limit*   Kathleen Norris, *Amazing Grace: A Vocabulary of Faith* (New York: Riverhead, 1998), 230.

127   *Anne Lamott tells*   Anne Lamott, *Traveling Mercies: Some Thoughts on Faith* (New York: Pantheon, 2000), 84.

Chapter Fourteen: Cooking, Listening, and Marriage

133   *Wisdom is not gained*   Barbara Brown Taylor, *An Altar in the World*, 14.

The willingness   Brené Brown, *Daring Greatly: How the Courage to Be Vulnerable Transforms the Way We Live, Love, Parent, and Lead* (New York: Gotham, 2012), 42.

139   *We cultivate love*   Brené Brown, *The Gifts of Imperfection: Let Go of Who You Think You're Supposed to Be and Embrace Who You Are* (Center City, MN: Hazelden, 2010), 26.

Chapter Fifteen: Humility, Prayer, and a Crazy-Quilt Pot Pie

144   *The miracle is*   Thich Nhat Hanh, *Thich Nhat Hanh: Essential Writings*, ed. Robert Ellsberg (Boston: Orbis, 2001), 23.

Sometimes when you need   Anne Lamott, *Traveling Mercies*, 167.

148   *a habitual, silent*   Brother Lawrence, *The Practice of the Presence of God: With Spiritual Maxims* (Grand Rapids, MI: Revell, 1999), 36.

Chapter Sixteen: Hospitality, Soup Kitchens, and Lenten Dinners

156   *Special attention*   John McQuiston II, *Always We Begin Again*, 61.

160   *There's a hunger*   Sara Miles, *Take This Bread: A Radical Conversion* (New York: Ballantine Books, 2007), 23.

163   *Our lives are inextricably bound*   Barbara Brown Taylor, *An Altar in the World*, 183.

Chapter Seventeen: Widows, Orphans, Deep Gladness, and Nest Fluffing

168   *The homes I like*   Martha Stewart, "Martha Stewart Is Editing Your Life (That Includes You, Bill Gates)," *Wired*, accessed January 18, 2017, https://www.wired.com/2003/06/home-spc/.

172   *The place God calls*   Frederick Buechner, "The Alphabet of Life," *ThirdWay* 17, no. 5 (June 1994): 24.

176   *My heart for her*   "Grace's Prayer," Etsy, accessed January 18, 2017, https://www.etsy.com/listing/155365171/graces-prayer.

Resources

The One, Inc., and Kathryn's House: theoneinc.org

The Green House Project: thegreenhouseproject.org

Kid President: kidpresident.com

Modern Farmer: modernfarmer.com

The House of Belonging: thehouseofbelonging.com

Sublime Stitching: sublimestitching.com

Jerusalem Greer: jerusalemgreer.com

About the Author

Jerusalem is a writer, speaker, minister, and farm-gal novice. She lives in Central Arkansas with her husband, Nathan, their two sons, and a host of critters. Together they are attempting to live a slower, more sacred version of modern life, right where they are.

To contact Jerusalem regarding speaking, writing, or hosting workshops, to read her blog, or to download discussion guides for *At Home in This Life,* visit http://www.JerusalemGreer.com.

To purchase Jerusalem's first book, *A Homemade Year: The Blessings of Cooking, Crafting, and Coming Together*, visit paracletepress.com.

Projects and Recipes

Acknowledgments

This book is not the book I set out to write when I pitched it four years ago, but it is the story that wanted to be told, lessons I needed to put down on paper so I would be able to visit them time and time again, because honestly, they are the lessons I think I will spend the rest of my life learning.

Learning, living, and book writing are all both incredibly solitary and communal endeavors. Which is why I always have so many people to thank, and I am sure I am going to forget so many, so please forgive me in advance.

Thank you to Aaron Reddin, whose work with The One, Inc., continues to teach me what it means to love my neighbor wholeheartedly. Thank you to the church communities who have led and loved me well across the journey chronicled in this book, specifically R Street Community Church in Little Rock and St. Luke's Episcopal Church in North Little Rock.

Thank you to my extended family and friends who all, in some way, at some point, pitched in and got their hands dirty during this season—scraping paint, planting shrubs, hanging wallpaper, or wiping away my tears. I love you all so much, and I wish you would just stop fighting the inevitable and move next door.

Thank you to my brother Joshua for letting me share some of his story. You have been challenging me and teaching me since the day you were born—I love you dearly.

I have to thank the community of women writers who I am honored to know, learn from, lean on, and be cheered on by. Thank you to Shauna, Sarah, Shannan, Tsh, Micha, Christie, Katherine, Osheta, Traci, Lisa, Sophie, and Rachel. Y'all make this process so much more fun, and a lot less lonely. Plus, you are all just dang brilliant women. Keep telling your truth!

Thank you to my family at St. Peter's Episcopal Church, Conway. Your love, support, and encouragement is the earth that grounds me. You are a beautiful example of what it means to love your neighbor as yourself, and I am honored to serve beside you.

To my extended church families—The Practice Tribe and Vintage Fellowship—thank you for letting me crash your parties and inviting me around your tables.

Thank you to Rev. Dr. Teri Daily—my priest, my boss, my friend, the person I am always learning from. I couldn't have done this without you. Let's go to Toad Suck Bucks and celebrate, okay?

I also have to give a huge shout-out to Alison Chino and Christine Archer, my back pocket editors, who are willing to do the dirty work of cleaning up my grammar and sentence structure (a major task). And I have to especially thank Christine, who will always tell me the hard truth. You make me a better writer.

Thank you to Jessica Bejot who makes me look good on the Web and whose talent knows no bounds. Thank you for cheering me on and for always being ready to dream big together!

Big thanks to the team at Paraclete Press, especially Phil Fox Rose, Mary Jordan, Sr. Antonia, and Karen Minster. Y'all put up with a lot of questions from me and are always willing to try new things, and I am so grateful for you all.

And thank you to my boys, Wylie and Miles. Being your mother is one of my greatest joys and challenges (the good kind!). You are wise, creative, loving young men, and it is an honor to call you my sons. I love you more than you will ever know.

And finally, thank you to Nathan. My partner, my love. Thank you for being willing to make yourself at home in this life of ours, in the beauty and the mess. I am a better person, and it is a wonderful life, because I share it with you.

About Paraclete Press

Who We Are

Paraclete Press is a publisher of books, recordings, and DVDs on Christian spirituality. Our publishing represents a full expression of Christian belief and practice—from Catholic to Evangelical, from Protestant to Orthodox.

We are the publishing arm of the Community of Jesus, an ecumenical monastic community in the Benedictine tradition. As such, we are uniquely positioned in the marketplace without connection to a large corporation and with informal relationships to many branches and denominations of faith.

What We Are Doing

PARACLETE PRESS BOOKS | Paraclete publishes books that show the richness and depth of what it means to be Christian. Although Benedictine spirituality is at the heart of all that we do, we publish books that reflect the Christian experience across many cultures, time periods, and houses of worship. We publish books that nourish the vibrant life of the church and its people.

We have several different series, including the best-selling Paraclete Essentials and Paraclete Giants series of classic texts in contemporary English; Voices from the Monastery—men and women monastics writing about living a spiritual life today; award-winning poetry; best-selling gift books for children on the occasions of baptism and first communion; and the Active Prayer Series that brings creativity and liveliness to any life of prayer.

MOUNT TABOR BOOKS | Paraclete's newest series, Mount Tabor Books, focuses on the arts and literature as well as liturgical worship and spirituality, and was created in conjunction with the Mount Tabor Ecumenical Centre for Art and Spirituality in Barga, Italy.

PARACLETE RECORDINGS | From Gregorian chant to contemporary American choral works, our recordings celebrate the best of sacred choral music composed through the centuries that create a space for heaven and earth to intersect. Paraclete Recordings is the record label representing the internationally acclaimed choir Gloriæ Dei Cantores, praised for their "rapt and fathomless spiritual intensity" by *American Record Guide*; the Gloriæ Dei Cantores Schola, specializing in the study and performance of Gregorian chant; and the other instrumental artists of the Arts Empowering Life Foundation.

Paraclete Press is also privileged to be the exclusive North American distributor of the recordings of the Monastic Choir of St. Peter's Abbey in Solesmes, France, long considered to be a leading authority on Gregorian chant.

PARACLETE VIDEO | Our DVDs offer spiritual help, healing, and biblical guidance for a broad range of life issues including grief and loss, marriage, forgiveness, facing death, bullying, addictions, Alzheimer's, and spiritual formation.

Learn more about us at our website:
www.paracletepress.com or phone us
toll-free at 1.800.451.5006

SCAN
TO
READ
MORE

You may also be interested...

A Homemade Year
The Blessings of Cooking, Crafting, and Coming Together
Jerusalem Jackson Greer

978-1-61261-067-2 $21.00 Full color Paperback

Let *A Homemade Year* inspire you to discover new and creative ways to experience the rhythm of God's story in your home, with your family and friends, through fun, colorful crafts, party ideas, and recipes. Divided into seasons, *A Homemade Year* is filled with celebrations that you already observe and some you may never have heard of. May this book be a jumping-off point for creating joy and lasting memories through the church year.

"This book is an absolute treasure. I want to share it with everyone I know!"
—REE DRUMMOND, #1 New York Times best-selling author of *The Pioneer Woman Cooks*

Everbloom
Stories of Deeply Rooted and Transformed Lives
Women of Redbud Writers Guild

978-1-61261-933-0 $18.99 Paperback

Be inspired by the transforming power of story.
Through the pain, loss, beauty and redemption in these pages, you'll find freedom in Christ and the courage to embrace your own story. The women of Redbud know the importance of spiritual shelter, and how easy it becomes to feel alone and misunderstood. In the *Everbloom* collection they offer essays, stories, and poetry: intensely personal accounts of transformation, and the journeys to find their own voices. Best of all, they invite you to join them, with writing prompts that encourage a response of honesty, faith, and imagination. Accept the invitation: set out on the journey to find your own voice.

"We read to see elements of our own hearts, experiences and stories reflected back to us in the words of others. This collection is just that: stories that help us feel seen, known, and understood. Honestly and beautifully told, this book will keep you in good company along your own journey."
—SHAUNA NIEQUIST, best-selling author of *Present Over Perfect*

Available through your local bookseller or through Paraclete Press:
www.paracletepress.com; 1-800-451-5006